THE COMING OF COAL

THE COMING OF COAL

ROBERT WALTER BRUÈRE

ISBN: 978-93-5614-433-0

Published: 1922

LECTOR HOUSE LLP
E-MAIL: lectorpublishing@gmail.com

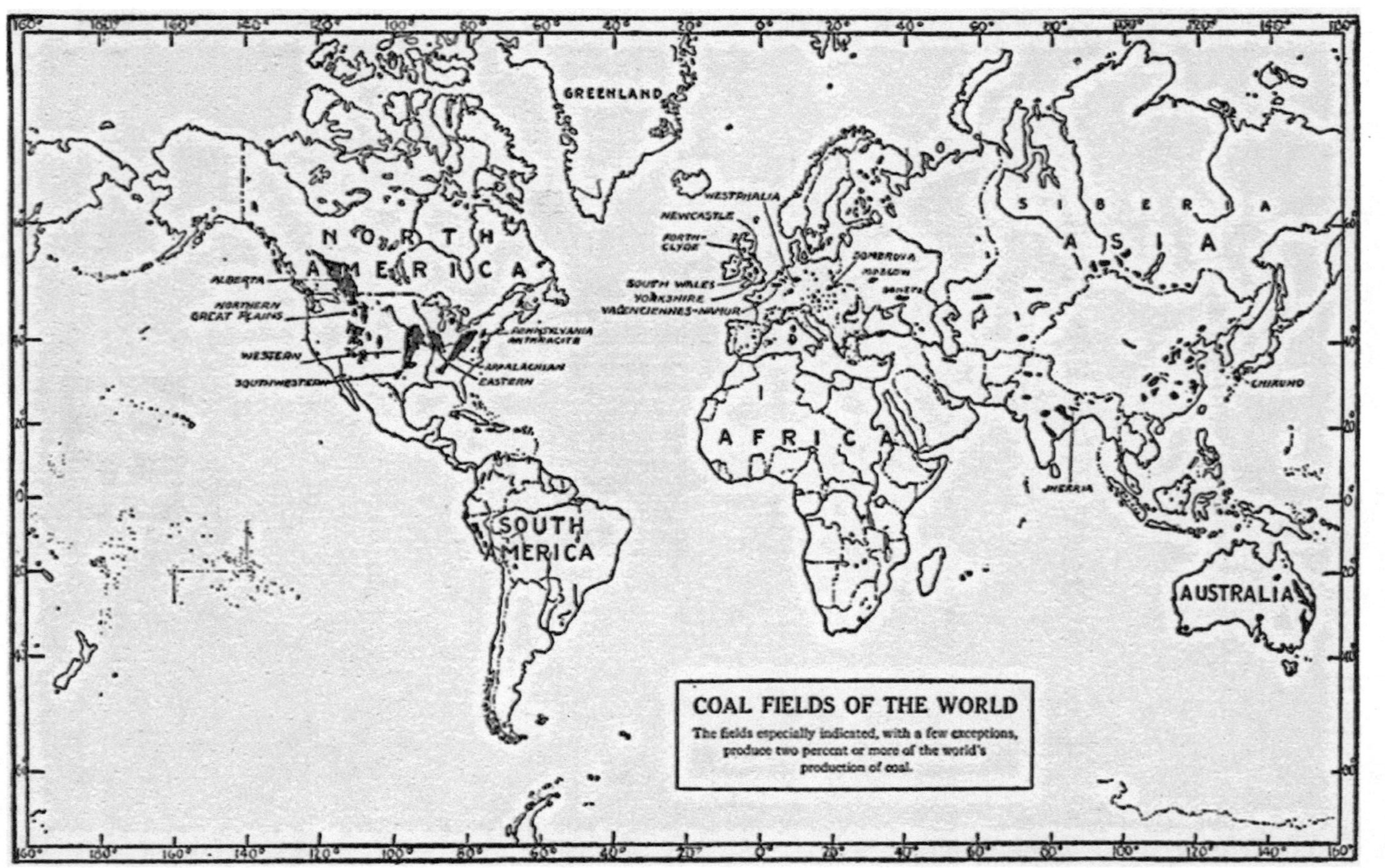

COAL FIELDS OF THE WORLD

THE COMING OF COAL

BY

ROBERT W. BRUÈRE
OF THE BUREAU OF INDUSTRIAL RESEARCH

Prepared for
The Educational Committee of the
Commission on the Church and Social Service
of the
Federal Council of the Churches of Christ in America

1922

FOREWORD

This book, important in subject and scientific in method, appears under religious auspices for a very definite reason. The Educational Committee of the Federal Council of Churches has sought to find concrete expression for those Christian principles which are too often confined to abstract statement. Christian ethics are well understood in theory. There is need now for a science of Christian conduct through which we may realize ethical ideals in our working life.

Because of its basic character and its present importance in the public mind the coal industry offers a field for this endeavor. Hence the Educational Committee presents through the medium of the Press of the Young Men's Christian Association, this book, addressed particularly to the people of the churches of America.

The Educational Committee.

CONTENTS

CHAPTER I

THE CHALLENGE OF POWER

Scientists tell us that the energy poured by the sun on the Desert of Sahara in a single day exceeds by fourfold the energy stored in the annual production of all the coal fields in the world. They dream of a time when the radiant energy of the sun will be captured and turned to the uses of man. Then the wheels of our myriad machines will spin with the sun and the stars. In the soft whirr of their motors men will hear the music of the spheres.

When that time comes, will it signal the triumph of man's will over nature, the end of the brute struggle with hunger? Will it find our ideals of cooperation, service, and brotherhood ripe for practical application? Or will it mark a new intensification of the exploitation of man by men, of the clash of groups for power, of international wars for possession? Shall we have the spiritual capacity to match our technical achievement? Shall we know what we mean when we pray Thy Kingdom Come on Earth as IT IS in Heaven?

That prayer was old on the lips of men when a comparable gift was discovered. During ages without number the shifting seas and the slow-moving mountains had pressed down the sun's vintage in the coal beds of the earth. Less than two centuries ago the steam engine harnessed coal to the looms of England. With coal came iron and steel, and with steel and steam came the industrial revolution, its factories massed in cities, its railroads weaving manufacturing centers together, its steel ships and cables and telegraph wires unfolding and integrating the economic life of the world. In western Europe especially it converted an age-long economic deficit into an economic surplus. For the first time in human history it brought the possibility of the good life to every man's door. But it found men spiritually unprepared. The ancient bread hunger was still upon them. As in the tribal days men warred upon one another for food, so now they warred upon one another for coal and the incredible spawn of coal. For coal means food, clothing, houses, ships, railroads, newspapers, chemicals, and guns. With the coming of coal and coal-driven machinery the earth and the fullness thereof was unlocked for the service of man. There was not only the possibility of the good life for each but also of a noble, well-ordered civilization for all. But instead of establishing civilization on foundations of mutual aid, service, and brotherhood, men turned their cities into shambles of childhood, poverty was embittered, civil strife in mine, mill, and factory became endemic, wars on an unprecedented scale engaged nations and groups of nations. The World War and the famine and widespread desolation that followed gave tragic evidence of our spiritual unpreparedness.

Yet it would be as falsely sentimental to set up a golden age as a heightening background for the evils that came with coal as it would be to ignore or gloze over those evils. Economic insecurity, poverty, disease, wars, and blighted childhood are as old as human existence. The world is a better, richer, more vibrant, and thrilling abode since coal came than it was before. The indictment of our coal age can be justly based, not upon what it has destroyed, but rather upon what it has missed,—upon its spiritually blind, its bungling and inadequate use of a gift more magnificent than any allotted to man since grain was first sown to the harvest and ground at a mill. An indictment that involves all mankind is hardly an indictment at all. It is rather a confession of our common human limitations, a recognition of the tragic circumstances of our spiritual growth. It will be answered when we as individuals and nations and groups of nations, set ourselves to turn the wisdom of experience to account in building a civilization worthy of a world that moves through infinite space with the sun and the marching stars.

CHAPTER II

THE COMING OF COAL

The making of all the coal in the earth began when the sun hurled the earth into its orbit. Before there were vertebrates in the sea, or animals, or plants of any kind on land—fully one hundred and fifty million years ago—low foldings and depressions appeared on the earth where the Appalachian Mountains now are. Following the lines of what has become the Atlantic, vast ridges appeared. Ages later swamp forests grew in the intervening valleys, bearing and shedding the spores and thick, somber leaves still traceable in the lower carboniferous strata. In that time, a shallow sea covered what is now the Mississippi Valley in whose sludgy shoals more swamp forests grew. Along the inland seas and ocean beaches of Europe and Asia, the tides, the winds, and rains slowly spread the clay for still other swamp forests. When the lush plant life of the carboniferous age came out of the marshy ooze, it spread along the edges of the land, crept up the long estuaries between the rising and sinking hills and on into the landlocked seas. The rocks beneath and about these carboniferous forests rose and sank age through age, cycle through cycle. When they sank slowly, tangled morasses formed; when they sank rapidly, the inrushing water killed the plants and buried them under a covering of silt. When the rocky strata rose again, the swamp forests crept back to their old places, and again bore and shed their fernlike leaves, their spores and great scarred trunks upon the oozy bottom now scores or hundreds of feet above the level on which their ancestors had stood ages before.

Then, some seventy million years ago, a geographical revolution convulsed what is now northeastern America. The great trough running parallel to the Atlantic, where swamp forests had grown and died and grown again, gave way under the ever-increasing load. The ridges at its sides pressed in upon it, crumpled it into giant folds, broke it, pushed its shattered edges out in mighty over-thrusts, released molten rock to flow up and over its torn surface. The whole titanic mass was racked and twisted with pressure and heat until what had been a slowly subsiding sea-bottom, covered with decaying swamp vegetation, rose on the shoulders of the newborn Appalachian Mountains, then a lofty range of clean, stark peaks stretching from Newfoundland to Arkansas,—two thousand miles.

And with this great geographical revolution, the work of making coal in eastern North America was finished. From the softest bituminous to the hardest anthracite, that work was done.

But in other parts of the world, the dense carboniferous forests continued to grow for another fifty or more million years. In the shallows of the Mississippi Valley, on the shores of the island that is now Colorado, the coal plants grew and died with the seasonal march of the sun. In parts of Europe, Russia, and China, coal continued to form.

And then came another geographical revolution, some twenty million years ago, that raised up the Rockies and the Andes along the western border of the Americas, tore and twisted and upturned the rocks of Europe and Asia, until with the exception of a few odd pockets where small swamp forests lived on for a time, the coal making of the whole earth was ended.

Twenty million years ago, all the coal we have or shall have had been packed away beneath the ribs of the earth, in seams varying in height from sixty feet to the thickness of a blade of grass. In many places the flat layers in which it was first deposited had been thrown into overlapping folds. Some of it had been subjected to comparatively little heat and to the pressure only of the rocky strata above it; this is the bituminous, which is still rich in oils, gas, tar—unreleased volatile matter. Some had been crushed by the weight of uplifted mountains, roasted, fused, and burned by molten lava and volcanic flame; this is anthracite, which is almost pure carbon and ash. Some had been exposed to greater pressure still, to intenser heat; this is graphite, which can no longer be burned at all.

The distribution of coal in the world by quality and quantity has been, next to climate and the fertility of the soil, the physical fact of most decisive importance in the history of modern civilization. For countless ages coal lay practically unused in the earth. Then, sometime between 1750 and 1760, an intricate interlocking of circumstances set coal to rule the world, not through new discoveries of coal itself but rather through improvements in spinning and weaving machinery which made possible the massing of large numbers of spinners and weavers for large-scale production if power could be found to drive the new machines for them. The steam engine had already been invented, but it was still a tentative thing, a primitive type, wondered at and experimented with. Coal had been used, but only in a few favored spots where it cropped out on the earth's surface, or was washed ashore by the sea, and then only as a domestic fuel. It was at the call of the master weavers and spinners of England that the steam engine was set to run the machines; then to furnish a blast so that coal might be used to cheapen the smelting of iron and steel so that more machines might be made; then to pump out the deepening mines so that more and more power to keep the machines running might be won. Steam raising was coal's first great play for power and it is the work through which it still holds its industrial supremacy. Between 1800 and 1900 coal-driven engines multiplied until by the end of the century they were producing energy equivalent to seventy million horse-power; during the first twenty years of the twentieth century, their power-producing capacity more than doubled. So coal wrought the industrial revolution, the greatest revolution in all human history, which transformed social and economic life as radically as the geographical revolution transformed the earth's surface.

"It introduced a new race of men," writes H. de B. Gibbins, "men who work with machinery instead of with their hands, who cluster together in cities instead of spreading over the land, men who trade with those of other nations as readily as with those of their own town, men whose workshops are moved by the great forces of nature and whose market is no longer the city or country but the world itself."

Measured by the crude standards of gross wealth and numbers, the people of the earth have flourished mightily since the dominion of coal began. The aggregate wealth of the world has increased to fabulous proportions. The average expectation of life among Western peoples has doubled. Between 1800 and 1910 the world's population rose from approximately 640,000,000 to 1,616,000,000. The population of England, which had increased only fifteen per cent from 1651 to 1751, increased two hundred per cent during the next century. Between 1816 and 1910, the population of France increased fifty per cent, of Germany three hundred per cent, of the United States seventeen hundred per cent.

Moreover the drive of coal's energy immensely stimulated men's inventive faculties. It transformed Kay's "flying shuttle" and Hargreaves' "spinning jenny" from clever toys into instruments of large-scale production, the crude steam engines of Newcomen and Watt into the great modern locomotive and the turbine engine; it made possible the large-scale production of telegraph wires and ocean cables, the cylinder press and typesetting machines, the electrical dynamo, the internal-combustion engine, the aeroplane, and even the space-ranging modern telescope. It lifted the veil from the seven seas, broke down the physical barriers between the peoples of the earth, forged the steel framework of national and international government. The commercial and political primacy which England held for more than one hundred and fifty years rested upon her abundant fields of easily accessible coal. The cosmic energy flowing out from her mines spread her trade and her surplus population to the four corners of the earth and made her triumphant over Spain and Holland—nations poor in coal. The coal of Westphalia, associated with the iron ores of Lorraine, welded the States of Germany into the empire of the latter nineteenth century and hurled her green-grey armies across her frontiers in the mad adventure of 1914. The vast, rich coal fields of North America have transformed the United States from an agricultural appanage of Europe into the foremost manufacturing and commercial nation in the world. The future of Russia lies largely in the coal fields of the Donetz basin. The imperfectly surveyed coal and ore fields of China and Siberia are probably the strongest of the magnets drawing the Powers into the problem of the Pacific. Coal and the continuing industrial revolution are still shaping the destiny of mankind.

But in the history of the human race the fact of transcending significance is the presence in man of instincts, emotions, mind, reason, will, conscious hunger, and conscious love of one's neighbor,—all the constituents of that personality of supreme worth whose ceaseless struggle for mastery over the forces of nature, for escape from hunger, want, and war into a world of plenty, beauty, mutual aid, and service is the epic of civilization. The value of coal, as of all material things, finds its true measure not in numbers or horse-power units, but in its effect upon the soul of man, the fullness of opportunity enjoyed by each individual for self-realization and service, the progress of the race toward brotherhood. The ultimate appraisal of the coal age will be determined by the issue of the struggle between bread hunger and love in the soul of man—the struggle between his acquisitive instinct and his growing consciousness of kind.

CHAPTER III
THE DRAMA OF CIVILIZATION

Coal embodies our chance of a world civilization. It is the material form in which the possibility of peace and ease, beauty and learning, cooperation and brotherhood, have come to the human race.

Before coal was harnessed to the looms of England, before the stored energy of the sun replaced hand labor at the wheels and gears of her newly invented machines, there was no such thing as a world civilization. There was indeed nothing to base a world civilization upon, for civilization implies leisure consciously to cooperate with other people, to make life not merely endurable but beautiful and pleasant as well, leisure to subordinate the instinct to acquire to the instinct to enjoy, the acquisitive instinct to the consciousness of kind—and the race as a whole had its entire attention focussed on the effort to get enough food and clothing and shelter so that it would live and not die. For only as the acquisitive instinct was dominant and successful could men survive either singly or in groups, before the coming of coal.

The limits of civilization were primarily the mechanical limitations of man's ability to produce. So long as his only ways to drive machinery were by wind and water, the strength of domesticated animals, and his own brawn, it was almost impossible for him to accumulate sufficient reserves of food and clothing so that instead of thinking what he should eat and what he should put on, he could think a little of how to make life good. And whenever by some fortunate chance a group of men did get together a small hoard, parallel with the growth of each tiny surplus grew the hatred of the outside groups who wished to possess it, and the need to defend it by force. So that when here and there through the centuries pocketed civilizations did arise, they were civilizations perpetually armed for defence and with the sword in their hands. And though the spirit of man in such places as India and Egypt, in China, Persia, Palestine, Greece, Carthage, Rome, and the free Italian cities, as soon as the pressure was removed ever so little, did flower into religion and art and science, these favored oases were surrounded by crowding, hungry multitudes who pressed in and in till at last every one of these was overwhelmed.

Before the coming of coal man had to satisfy his longing for peace and knowledge and companionship through his dreams. These have come down to us in the legends of India and Israel, China, Greece, and our own Nordic ancestors which perpetually play about the fabulous treasure—the Golden Fleece, the land of milk and honey, the Volsung's miraculous hoard—pathetic symbols of plenty, liberation, and the possibility of brotherhood. But until coal came there was no way to make these dreams come true. For survival was only to the strong, or to the cunning, or to those who were willing to grow fat on the leanness of others, and every respite from the basic business of keeping alive was extravagantly paid for either by oneself or another—before coal came.

But with the coming of coal there rose the possibility of producing more than enough to keep everybody alive. A tireless bond servant had been given to the race whose power grew as it was called on, until now in the United States where coal is used most indefatigably, each family has the equivalent of thirty human servants, whose use does not need to involve the exploitation of man by man. For the first time there is the possibility of all having enough,—of a world surplus on which to base civilization.

It was too much to expect that this possibility should be understood by a race which had never before got further than to see that if their family, their town, their nation, was to have ease and plenty, it must be quick to get as much of the world's store of food and goods as it could,—and to acquire them in spite of the fact that the other groups, who were hot after them also, might perish if they did not get their share. They did not see that with the coming of coal the supply was practically unlimited, and so it was not man's sense of brotherhood but his acquisitive instinct, checked and balked for ages, that first found channels of release when coal came.

After the coming of coal this acquisitive instinct expanded with cosmic force. For the first time in history, men and nations thrilled with the manifest possibility of their escape from the ancient menace of hunger into a world of measureless plenty. In their greedy rush for possession, men within nations trampled one another under foot, and nations girded themselves for world dominion. And as wealth flowed into the village, the town, and the nation, all men exulted, those who themselves had nothing as well as those who grew rich. For famine still hovered beyond the horizon, and the very presence in the community of an economic surplus, by whomever owned, gave all men a sense of security as though at last they had won the miraculous hoard of their dreams, through the coming of coal.

It was inevitable that in this cumulative drive of the acquisitive instinct with the long-sought surplus almost in sight, the attitude of mind established and glorified during the ages when war was the common alternative to hunger, should carry over into factories and mines. The methods of war,—the ruthless sacrifice of part of the community for the benefit of the rest,—were the only methods men understood. The new possibility had arrived but the old habit of mind remained. With the coming of coal and the beginning of the industrial revolution, no one dreamed that the time for the cessation of human sacrifice had arrived. When the mines were first opened, the slave trade still flourished with almost universal sanction.

"It is a slight fact," wrote Lecky, "but full of ghastly significance as illustrating the state of feeling at the time, that the ship in which Hawkins sailed on his second expedition to open the English slave trade was called *The Jesus.*"

This voyage was made a hundred years before the harnessing of coal, but in the middle of the eighteenth century and far into the nineteenth much the same state of feeling widely prevailed. The first miners in Scotland were serfs; the first miners in northern England were bondsmen who sold themselves by the year and were forbidden by law to leave the mine to which they were bound.

"At that time," write J. L. and Barbara Hammond, basing their account on the report of the Parliamentary Committee on the Employment of Children and Young Persons (1842), "boys were employed everywhere, girls in certain districts, Lancashire, Cheshire, the West Riding, and South Wales, besides Scotland. Children were employed as trappers, that is to open and shut the doors that guided the draught of air through the mine; as fillers, that is to fill the skips and carriages when the men have hewn the coal; and as pushers, or hurriers, that is, to push the trucks along from the workers to the foot of the shaft. But in some mines these trucks were drawn instead of being pushed. 'A girdle is put round the naked waist, to which a chain from the carriage is hooked and passed between the legs, and the boys crawl on their hands and knees, drawing the carriage after them.' In the early days of the century this arrangement was very common, and women and girls were so employed. By 1842 it was more usual to have small iron railways, and the carriages were pushed along them. The trapping was done everywhere by children, generally from five to eight years of age. A girl of eight years old described her day: 'I'm a trapper in the Gamber Pit. I have to trap without a light, and I'm scared. I go at four and sometimes half-past three in the morning and come out at five and half-past. I never go to sleep. Sometimes I sing when I've light, but not in the dark; I dare not sing then....' In the West Riding the work of hurrying or pushing the corves was often done by girls at the time of the report: 'Chained, belted, harnessed like dogs in a go-cart, black, saturated with wet, and more than half naked—crawling upon their hands and feet, and dragging their heavy loads behind them—they present an appearance indescribably disgusting and unnatural.' ... The children who suffered most were the apprentices from the workhouse; 'these lads are made to go where other men will not let their own children go. If they will not do it, they take them to the magistrates who commit them to prison.' ... In mines with thick seams it was usual to make good roads, but in less profitable mines the roads were just large enough to enable small children to get the corves along them.... It was reported that there was much more cruelty in the Halifax pits than in those of Leeds and Braseford. A sub-commissioner met a boy crying and bleeding from a wound in the cheek, and his master explained 'that the child is one of the slow ones, who would only move when he saw blood, and that by throwing a piece of coal at him for that purpose he had accomplished his object, and that he often adopted the like means.'"

The entire community sanctioned these practices, not the employers only; for generations even the miners themselves acquiesced in them. Those who were sacrificed in the mines and factories were victims of the entire consuming community's war against hunger; the furious drive of the acquisitive instinct on the one hand, and also of the passionate longing of all men to escape from economic bondage into security, plenty, economic and spiritual freedom. It was war of a disastrous sort but the world of that day saw no alternative,—could see no alternative from the experience of the race. Until as individuals, and nations and associations of nations, we have won a stable economic surplus and the spiritual maturity to use and distribute that surplus for the benefit of the whole community, we shall not in our hearts condemn war as immoral, whether it be a military or an industrial war. Always we shall contrive to believe that what is necessary for us is necessarily good.

People in general deplored the horrors of mining just as before the coming of coal they had deplored the horrors of the wars they had waged in order to survive, but the fact remained that if the golden promise of the industrial revolution was to be realized they must have coal, and what other way was there to get it? At least part of the world was living in comfort and security.

As a matter of fact a fair share of the community attained reasonable comfort after the coming of coal. The acquisitive instinct succeeded in piling up a vast permanent capital which was enjoyed by a large proportion of the human race. It had not come through increased production alone. Raiding and exploitation, both commercial and military, had helped mightily, for the old method of feeding yourself from your neighbor's hoard was tremendously accelerated for those peoples whose manufactures and transportation were driven by the power of coal. That the exploited peoples suffered in proportion as the raiding peoples prospered is, of course, true, but among the dominant peoples themselves the acquisitive instinct had begotten a mutual consciousness. Throughout those parts of the world where coal had induced the industrial revolution, a common civilization had sprung up. Parallel with the triumphant acquisitive instinct had developed the spirit of brotherhood and mutual aid which limited and controlled it. The feeling of fellowship which breeds civilization was practically coextensive with the augmented surplus produced through the coming of coal. Coal-driven transportation was good enough so that a famine in one land could be met by the heavy crops from another place: the fighting of disease, the utilization of patents, the exchange of ideas, of luxuries, of scientific knowledge, of passports, of fashions, and of food, became international throughout a large part of the world. Mankind began to approach a world civilization because since the coming of coal to kill or starve was no longer the inevitable choice.

That this alternative has even a chance of operating is due to the play and interplay of the two great fundamental instincts in the soul of man—the acquisitive instinct through which he learned to use coal to pile up the material surplus that made civilization possible; and that other impulse, an offspring of the acquisitive instinct, which has swung into opposition to its parent but without whose help that parent could never have achieved a surplus on a large scale, the instinct of brotherhood, of mutual aid, of cooperation. For without cooperation among men there would have been lacking the tremendous advantage of division of labor and mass production, and no surplus, however large and secure it might have been, could have resulted in civilization except through mutual aid. Men learned to work together in order to survive; they learned to enjoy the results of their labor together in order to become civilized. These two impulses are woven together in man's history from the start and it is according as one or the other predominates that we develop a civilization on the basis of our economic surplus, or merely continue to exist and fight. This instinct of mutual aid is as truly a cosmic force as the acquisitive instinct.

"The original and elementary subjective fact in society is the consciousness of kind," writes Professor Giddings, "… It is the basis of class distinction, of innumerable forms of alliance, of rules of intercourse, and of peculiarities of policy…. It is about the consciousness of kind as a determining principle, that all other motives organize themselves in the evolution of social choice, social volition, or social policy."

In any attempt to understand the function of coal in the development of human society, it is necessary to remember the universal democratic tendency of men similarly circumstanced, to organize into defensive and offensive groups. They organize into bar associations, medical societies, religious denominations, manufacturers' associations, and trade unions in obedience to a principle as pervasive in the animate as the force of gravitation is in the material world. While the primary driving force behind each group as it organizes is the acquisitive instinct, the natural reaching out for the means of subsistence, for wages, fees, profits; for food, clothing, shelter, then for more food, more clothing, better shelter, still the actual attainment of the surplus makes possible the widening operation of the consciousness of kind, and turns men's minds toward all those attributes that are characteristic of the good life in which both the individual personality and also the spiritual being of the group, the nation, and the race find fruition. For an economic surplus is merely the condition of the good life, and the end to which the human spirit forever strives to direct the use of the surplus, is the good life itself—a worthy civilization.

If the consciousness of kind had spread evenly like a rising tide drawn by the swelling surplus of the age of coal, a world civilization might have quickly come. But it worked unevenly and erratically. Sometimes it spread thinly over whole nations in the form of political beliefs and produced theoretical democracies functioning through the franchise. Sometimes it left the forms of government severely monarchical and produced a spotty economic growth in the form of cooperative societies that functioned in response to the everyday bread and butter needs. Sometimes it brought those having similar occupations together in guilds and trade unions, that tended to ignore mere political boundaries and make men internationally conscious of each other through the way they got their living. But everywhere the rising consciousness of kind came upon obstructions and divisions. Waves hurrying up innocent-looking estuaries would come upon other streams from the same great source, and meet in spluttering, frothing conflict: a long even swell of brotherly feeling would break over some rock of ancestral race prejudice in disaster and bloodshed; mutual aid rose in a murky troubled sea, wave against wave, one current trying to beat another current back. People united into a political nation opposed themselves violently to those united into some economic class within it. Men were driven apart when the interests of their group conflicted with the interests of other groups almost as strongly as they were drawn together by common interest within their own organization.

And always the rise of any new group within a fairly comfortable community met opposition from some already established group whose privileges, powers, and possessions the new group tended to infringe. They inevitably appeared like an invading tribe bent on pillage, and the community gathered shoulder to shoulder to resist them, every thought and muscle set to repel what they saw as an attack on the common surplus and in defence of those whose guardianship of the common hoard had afforded them a new measure of comfort.

This has been particularly true of all organizations, due to the spread of consciousness of kind among the workers and their efforts to get for themselves a larger share of the benefits of the common surplus. Very rarely has the community been able to see that what was distributed in the form of advanced wages and better conditions was not necessarily taken away from the community as a whole.

When the coal miners, actuated by the consciousness of kind, began to organize for mutual aid and defence, the community at large as well as the mine owners condemned them as subversive conspirators, not only against their lawful masters, but also against the general peace and well-being of the nation, which was quite obviously flourishing,—piling up a surplus with national security as a by-product,—by reason of the thousands of tons of coal which the newly organized group might conceivably curtail. It was the community as a whole, not the employers only, that sanctioned the use of the courts and the military against the miners' union, as they would have countenanced their use against soldiers who mutinied.

Only slowly is our community, to which the coming of coal has given the chance to develop a world civilization, beginning to see that neither the acquisitive instinct through which men pile up a surplus, nor the consciousness of kind through which they organize to build up a civilization, is the result of individual perversity or caprice. Unions and employers' associations arise in obedience to a fundamental law of human conduct, they are the means by which society wins its way out of chaos and anarchy into peace and orderly government. Through such group organizations men develop the understanding of one another and of the community at large, which is the foundation of brotherhood and civilized life. It is through them that the community develops standards of living; it is through them that the ideals of cooperation acquire reality. It is by the acquisitive instinct that men live; it is by the consciousness of kind, the instinct of mutual aid and cooperation, that men are transformed into human beings. The interplay of these forces makes the history of civilization—of nations and the great basic industries within the nations. They are the flying shuttles with which man at Time's loom weaves "the living garment of God."

CHAPTER IV
COAL IN AMERICA

The human significance of coal lies in the effect which the release of its energy has exercised upon the struggle between the acquisitive instinct and the consciousness of kind for ascendancy over the soul of man. Through its creature, the industrial revolution, it has given man command of an economic surplus and set him free to win the good life for each individual and to substitute mutual aid for war in international relations if he will.

But the first effect of coal was not to usher in the good life but to intensify the ancient struggle, widening its stage from pocketed civilizations to the world. For more than a hundred and fifty years, the abundant and readily accessible coal of Great Britain made her the protagonist in the world drama. Her acquisitive instinct, charged with cosmic energy, shot lines of imperial expansion out across the seas to America, India, Australia, China, and Africa. Her coal-created wealth enabled her to maintain the mastery of the ocean highways which she had won from Spain and Holland and to hold it against Napoleonic France and later against imperial Germany. It gave her an economic surplus upon the basis of which the consciousness of kind welded her people into one nation and ended the civil wars which from the time of the Danish invasion and the landing of William the Conqueror had kept each little group within the island armed against every other little group. And it transformed her with jarring rapidity into a country that lived by manufacture and by trade and supported a far larger population than could have lived upon the island if it had been merely an agricultural country raising its own food.

In order that this swelling population might go on getting coal out of the mines and turning out products from the factories it must be adequately and cheaply fed. The place where its food came from was chiefly America. During the hundred and fifty years of England's primacy, America was not only her granary but increasingly the granary of other nations, and the great reservoir for all their overflowing populations. For the industrial revolution in England was followed by the harnessing of coal in France, then in Germany, then later in Japan, and this set in motion among them the processes of imperial expansion, whose friction and clash culminated in the World War.

It was as necessary to the success of the industrial revolution, particularly in specialized little England, that the surplus populations which were poured by the million into America should send back food to Europe, as it was that their factory machines should have coal to drive them. This interdependence was not conscious, not a deliberate effort on either side, but it was an extremely practical fact nevertheless. In order that England might live by trade, some other land must live by agriculture, and during the first hundred and fifty years of the industrial revolution that land was America.

To live by agriculture was an easy thing in the New World, easier than it had ever been anywhere before,—to live and to feed a continent besides. For America is the only great modern nation whose history is written not against a background of famine but against a background of economic abundance. After the first thin stream of colonial adventurers and exiles for conscience' sake had established themselves upon the Atlantic coast, her seemingly boundless domain opened up before the hungry millions of Europe like the promised land of milk and honey. Unlike the peoples of the great Asiatic and European folk-wanderings, they found no comparably developed peoples to bar their way. As they spread from the Atlantic to the Blue Ridge and Alleghenies, then along the Great Lakes and down the Ohio; on across the Mississippi, the Kansas prairies, the Great Desert, the Sierras and Rockies to California and the Golden Gate, they found only hunting tribes or the fading remnants of cliff-dwelling and primitive agricultural clans. These they could meet not only with effective weapons of defence but also with a highly developed agricultural technique.

At first America's planless prosperity had little to do with coal and nothing at all with manufacture. It was a prosperity made up of the sum of her food products, and men skimmed the soil and the forests with only one thought, to make that sum immediately great. Exploitation got into their blood. It was the method by which they grew rich, and when the wealth of the coal deposits was added to the wealth of the fields and forests, they carried the same methods of planless exploitation over into the coal mines. England must still depend on them for food, but they did not have to depend so abjectly on her for manufactures after the industrial revolution crossed the Atlantic at the call of the Pennsylvania coal fields.

After the industrial revolution harnessed their unique reservoirs of coal, the people of the United States enjoyed a degree of economic security such as no other people ever enjoyed. Had they been spiritually prepared, they might have used this economic abundance to establish brotherhood among men. But after all, they themselves were Europeans who had fled from the ancient tyranny of hunger. To them America was naturally more an escape from that haunting menace than a challenge to the good life. Here and there, as in the Puritan theocracy, they heard and tried to obey the challenge. But they were not prepared.

The hungry immigrant millions swarmed across the continent, laying waste the forests, skimming the fresh fertile soil, growing prosperous by destruction rather than by thrift and planful use. They caroused and swaggered like prodigals. They glorified mere acquisition, measuring a man's worth by the money he owned. As they filled the continent, the old world fever of imperial expansion entered their blood. They seized Cuba and the Philippines, Haiti and Santo Domingo. They set about building the greatest navy in the world. After a few faltering efforts to lead the warring nations to peace through conference and conciliation, they threw the weight of their wealth and numbers into the balance and with fire and sword imposed a victorious peace. And they were able to do this in the last analysis because of the enormous power of their coal supply, for coal in a modern industrial civilization means guns and munitions of war, transportation systems to set armies in the field, and the ability to supply them after they get there. America's coal-wrought wealth made her decisive in battle. Even so today her unique reserves of coal make her the arbiter between peace and war. Possessed of the richest coal fields in the world, she holds the destiny of the nations in her hands. For coal has grown to mean food and clothing and shelter, transportation and communication, and the economic surplus and the leisure without which science, invention, art, representative government, democratic education, and enlightened organized religion would atrophy and perish.

Since coal means all these things, and since America owns the world's greatest available reserves of coal, it is obvious that the manner in which her people develop and govern their coal fields is of crucial importance, not only to themselves, but also to the rest of the world. Before the United States entered the World War, her people were hardly aware of this fact; even the momentous experience of the war has but dimly impressed its meaning upon the national mind.

Our coal measures underlie an area of more than four hundred and sixty thousand square miles. They contain almost four thousand billion tons of lignite, bituminous, semibituminous, anthracite, and semianthracite coals. About two-fifths of the world's annual output is mined in the United States.

The very abundance of the supply has made us enormously wasteful in its exploitation, as we have been wasteful in the exploitation of our forests. Unlike the forests, coal once destroyed does not grow again. The most valuable of our coals are in the Appalachian bituminous fields that stretch from northern Pennsylvania to Alabama, and in which some of the best sections have already been gutted and abandoned. In our greedy grasp for wealth, we have left one ton of coal to waste underground for every ton we have brought to the surface. More than one hundred and fifty thousand miners have been drawn into the mines in excess of efficient requirements. Planless overexpansion of the industry has resulted in such irregular operation of plant and equipment that for more than a generation the miners have lost an average of ninety-three days in the working year of three hundred and eight days, and a needless overhead charge has been imposed upon the consumer which Mr. F. G. Tryon of the U. S. Geological Survey calculates at a million dollars for each working day. Planless exploitation has made the most basic of our basic industries the prey of technical inefficiency and social unrest, the extent of which we as a people ignored until they threatened national and international disaster at the crisis of the war.

This trouble might have gone on some time longer undiagnosed if we had not met our first modern national emergency in 1917. Of necessity the weight of the military structure was added to the weight of the industrial civil structure and the combined load was more than the coal industry could bear. It bent and broke under it, and in order to prosecute the war, the government was forced to take hold of the formless inchoate thing and reshape it into a stable prop for the national need.

As a first step it was necessary to find out what this great unwieldy coal industry was.

Coal mines are systems of tunnels driven into the veins where they crop out along the slopes of hills, or from the foot of shafts sunk through the overlying strata. These tunnels run for miles underground. Secondary tunnels run from the main tunnel or heading into the rooms where the miners work. The surveyor's diagram of a mine looks like a crushed centipede. The getting of coal out of the mines, after it has been picked or blasted down by the miner, like its distribution after it is brought to the surface, is almost entirely a problem of transportation.

Even in times of peace our railroad transportation was an intricate and complicated thing. It had been repeatedly regulated and re-regulated to bring it more in line with community needs. Among other regulations was a law, designed to give the public the benefit of as much competition between operators as possible, which required the railroads to furnish sidings and cars to all coal mines in proportion to their production, with a preferential provision for new operations. The double demand for coal sent up prices and the rise in prices led to the opening of new coal mines and the re-working of old abandoned ones. All the eleven thousand mines, scattered more or less at random over thousands of square miles of territory, clamored for their legal quota of cars and transportation to market. This competitive din aggravated the confusion upon our already overtaxed railroads. At the critical moment when the essential movement of troops and munitions was straining the resources of the railroads, the sprawling coal industry made their task impossible.

In peace times one-third of our ordinary bituminous production is used to generate steam for transportation, and more than one-third of all the tonnage carried by the railroads is coal. The weight of the coal which the railroads normally carry is double the weight of iron ore, steel, lumber, wheat, corn, oats, and hay combined. The problem of hauling this huge load is needlessly complicated by competitive cross-shipments of coal from one mining state into or across another. The producers of Illinois, Pennsylvania, and Indiana sell their coal in from eighteen to twenty states, many of them coal-mining states. A part of this cross-shipment is necessary, because certain mining states like Illinois, for example, do not produce the grade of coking coal which their steel plants need and which must, therefore, be brought from West Virginia or southern Pennsylvania. But most of it is due to blind competitive planlessness and waste.

Upon this tangled mesh the critical demands of the war placed a crushing burden. The nation's safety made it imperative not only that coal should be produced, but that it should be delivered where it was needed. The miners were digging more coal than had ever been produced before, yet cries of coal shortage went up from domestic consumers and manufacturers all over the land. The railroads themselves resorted to the confiscation of coal in transit to keep their engines running. To avert impending catastrophe to the nation and the world, the national consciousness of kind asserted itself over the acquisitive instinct of individuals and groups, and through the federal government created the Fuel Administration which brought the mines under unified public control and converted the coal industry, for the period of the war, into a unified public service.

From the high central tower of the Fuel Administration, the people of the United States for the first time caught a fleeting glimpse of the coal industry as a whole and of the relation it bears to the national and international industrial life. They discovered that coal bears much the same relation to our modern industrial structure that the water supply bears to the life of a great municipality. When America entered the war, she resembled with respect to her primary source of mechanical energy a municipality dependent for its water supply upon eleven thousand separate wells, owned and operated primarily in their individual interests by thousands of enterprising individuals, with hundreds of separate delivery systems jostling in the highways that needed to be kept clear for soldiers and guns, its people bidding against one another, offering fabulous prices for water, yet parched with thirst.

"Basic industries and transportation," writes Dr. Garfield, in describing what he saw as head of the Fuel Administration, "were caught in a vicious circle. Steel could not be manufactured without coke, coke could not be made without coal; coal could not be commercially produced without transportation; transportation was dependent upon coal.... Industrially we were in a wild scramble of manufacture, production, and shipment.... It was no longer a question of withholding coal from non-war industries but rather a question whether any coal could much longer get through to any consumer."

With eleven thousand coal mines in operation, the engines of the nation were running cold for lack of coal.

Created to avert impending catastrophe, the Fuel Administration went about the service of the nation much as an engineer would tackle the job of converting eleven thousand wells into a modern system of water supply. It dealt with the coal fields as a single great reservoir of fuel and power. It worked out a budget covering the needs of the essential industries, the railroads, steel plants, munition factories, gas and electric utilities, as well as the domestic consumers. It made maps charting the coal-producing and coal-consuming territories, divided the nation into regional zones, established these zones as fuel reservoirs, created a distributing organization by zones and states like a great system of water mains. It called the experienced operators and technical managers into public service and entrusted to them the technical problems of production and distribution. It fixed prices limiting profits to an estimated fair return. It converted the miners' union and the operators' organizations into administrative arms of the government for the industry, with committees for conference and conciliation at the mines, and in the various producing districts, heading up in a Bureau of Labor at Washington as a final court of appeal for the adjustment of disputes over wages and working conditions.

For the period of the war, the coal industry functioned as a cooperative public service. The coal budget, based upon a detailed analysis of the country's resources and needs, set a definite standard of performance both for the industry and the railroads, and made it possible for them to cooperate intelligently. The zones served as tools for the control and direction of the flow of coal called for by the budget. Mr. C. E. Lesher, Director of the Bureau of Statistics of the Distribution Division, writes: "In the short period of a few months after the work of the Fuel Administration was begun, it was determined that the requirements of the United States for bituminous coal in the coal year ended March, 1919, were 624,000,000 net tons, compared with a production in 1917 of 552,000,000 tons of bituminous coal, and for anthracite 100,000,000 net tons, but slightly more than in 1917.... To provide coal was the problem of the Distribution Division of the Fuel Administration; to provide transportation was the problem of the Railroad Administration.... The adoption of the zoning system represented the supreme effort of the Railroad Administration to overcome the transportation tangle in connection with coal.... So closely did the officials of the two administrations work, and so effective were the measures employed, that the results surprised all.... The Director of Operations of the Railroad Administration in May, when production of bituminous coal was averaging 11,500,000 tons a week, believed that 11,800,000 was the highest that could be expected in 1918, as the railroads were believed to have reached their maximum capacity. Within a month records of 12,500,000 tons a week were reached, and in July, and again in September, the 13,000,000 ton mark was passed.... When the armistice was declared, New England, farthest from the mines, with an average of 20 weeks' supply, was literally gorged with soft coal, and eastern New York and Pennsylvania, with from 6 to 9 weeks' stock, had abundant supplies.... From April 1 to July 6, 1918, rail shipments to New England were 3,058,000 net tons, or 98 per cent of the schedule of 3,150,000 tons; on September 28, shipments were 6,164,000 tons, or 105 per cent of the schedule for that date. The schedule for shipments to tidewater from April 1 to July 1 called for 11,916,000 net tons. By December 21 shipments were 9 per cent ahead of the program. The Lake program called for 28,000,000 tons of cargo coal; a total of 28,153,000 tons was supplied. With similar precision and certainty munition factories, arsenals, powder works, and by-product plants were kept running, while stocks were accumulated, insuring uninterrupted operations throughout the winter. In the same manner retail dealers were given supplies for their domestic trade. Such results were possible only because of complete control of shipments and the full information on which to proceed."

This was an amazing and illuminating demonstration of the fact that our greatest national resource could be administered for the benefit of the whole nation. It was no longer a mere possibility, the thing had been done.

It has been said that this achievement was possible because during the war the people had a common object which so challenged their higher ideals that they were able to subordinate their individual and special group interests to the service of the nation, to make their consciousness of kind as a people triumphant over the acquisitive instinct. Again it is said that human nature being what it is, similar unselfish consecration is not to be expected in the sluggish days of peace. But if the historical record teaches us anything it is the essential falseness of this assertion. That record shows us the gradual irresistible spread of the consciousness of kind from one realm of human activity to another as the acquisition of a surplus makes this possible. It shows human understanding reaching out to give all men religious freedom, to assure them equal political rights; shows it asserting human brotherhood in the right to education, health, happiness—and these things not under the stress of war, but in the conditions of peace. The possibility hangs not on any technical inability, but on the better preparedness of the minds of men, on their clearer vision, their ability to see the spiritual implications of their technical triumphs.

CHAPTER V

THE AWAKENING OF THE MINERS

With the declaration of the armistice and the removal of the incentive to co-operation in public service which the war gave, the Fuel Administration and its elaborate system of statistical control of production and distribution was broken up as rapidly as it had been organized. During the war, there had been gross examples of profiteering just as there had been occasional local strikes, but by and large the operators like the miners had conducted themselves conscientiously as servants of the republic. To a remarkable degree they subordinated their acquisitive instinct to their consciousness of kind as citizens of the nation whose life was threatened from without. But within a year after the armistice, speculative profiteering was rampant and the coal industry was paralyzed by a general strike. Mr. Herbert Hoover, addressing the American Institute of Mining and Metallurgical Engineers, described the situation as a "national emergency," due to the fact that "this industry, considered as a whole, is one of the worst functioning industries in the United States."

How shall we account for this wide, swift swing of the pendulum? Operators and owners who had offered their skill to the government during the national crisis, rebelled against all further "interference with their private business." They rebelled not only against price fixing and the regulation of distribution, but even against all attempts on the part of governmental agencies to keep congress and the public informed of the elementary facts of ownership, costs, wages, prices, and profits, without which public opinion is helplessly blind. They sued out an injunction against the Federal Trade Commission to block its efforts to search out and publish these essential facts. The unions also chafed under governmental restraint upon their freedom of action, especially when the government lifted its limitation on prices and left the consumer at the mercy of an open market. As prices and profits mounted, they felt entitled to commensurate wage increases. The war, they said, was over though peace had not been formally declared, and they demanded release from the restraints of wartime legislation so that they might freely exercise their economic pressure to secure wage increases as the operators were taking increased profits. For the first time in almost a generation they laid down their tools, and finally submitted to the arbitration of federal commissions only under threat of an injunction and the imprisonment of their leaders. Economic war and group rivalry took the place of cooperation in public service.

The main reason for this violent reaction is probably to be found in the fact that our modern democracies, the United States in particular, were born in rebellion against the autocratic authority of the feudal state, the fear and hatred of which still attaches even to our representative government. The memory of the Stuarts and Bourbons and Hohenzollerns is still fresh in the modern democratic consciousness, and accounts for the maxim that the government is best which governs least. Through the revolutions of the eighteenth century the merchants, manufacturers, and business men wrested from the monarch his autocratic power, and it is against this same power as exercised by the owners of property that the organized labor movement is today in rebellion. But as against the state when it exercises such autocratic authority as during the war it exercised through the Fuel Administration, both groups, owners and workers, unite. They assert the right of self-government within their industry. Like the economists and business men of the nineteenth century, they contend that the conflict and balance of their selfish interests will by some mysterious provision of nature neutralize and resolve these selfishnesses to the advantage of the community. The essence of this acquisitive philosophy is expressed in the quaint nineteenth-century maxim that "greed is held in check by greed, and the desire for gain sets limits to itself." But this leaves the service of the community at the mercy of a blind conflict of forces within the industry, as formerly it was at the mercy of force exercised by the monarch who was the state, and the public is increasingly dissatisfied with the result. The public service conception of industry, and especially of such basic industries as coal, is rapidly taking possession of the public mind. People are coming to see that the uncontrolled conflict of forces, like autocratic force itself, is incompatible with the principle of service. Neither will force exercised by the state through the courts solve the difficulty. Compulsion is contrary to the spirit and genius of democracy. The great problem of our generation is to discover how industrial freedom can be reconciled with the service of the public. For an answer we shall have to look into the spirit and structure of such government as our industries have themselves evolved. For democracy is not, as its earlier critics declared, synonymous with anarchy. Democracy is a government of laws, not of men; and laws in a democracy are not emanations of superior minds, but the codified experience of the people.

As we approach the problem of government in our basic industries as in the nation, we discover two seemingly conflicting tendencies, two great elements in our population apparently pulling in opposite directions. In the question of national security and defence, the one instinctively follows the ancient tradition of European nations, piling up armies and navies, and striving to make America the most formidable military power in the world; the second leans to a policy of reconciliation, striving by conference and understandings with other nations to prevent disagreements and to avert wars. The first makes it a matter of national honor to emphasize individual American rights on land and sea, the property rights of Americans, our financial and economic interests in backward countries, and the military force necessary to enforce those interests; the second aims to establish international relations in which such rights and interests shall be secure to all nations without the constant threat of force. To the one, the world is an arena in which to fight or starve is the eternal choice; to the second, the world is a communion table at which all men are brothers.

These same tendencies, these same manifestations of the acquisitive instinct and the consciousness of kind, appear in the record of our basic coal industry. As the industrial revolution got into full swing in America, during and immediately following the Civil War, there was a rush for the possession of the coal mines comparable to the rush for land. Among the men who won possession, there were some who were keenly aware of the public obligations of ownership, who in friendly cooperation with their employes strove to develop their properties in the interest of the public as well as of their employes and themselves. But owners and miners alike took their spiritual color from their social environment and in the soul of the people the acquisitive instinct remained in the ascendant. Men did not go into business or swing their tools for their health. Their first duty, as they saw it, was to make all the money they could as fast as they could, and to put themselves and those dependent upon them on easy street. "God helps them," they said, "who help themselves." They gutted the richest veins for quick profit, as our forests and new lands had been gutted. More mines were opened than the nation could possibly use. There was a gluttonous overdevelopment of the industry which swung up and down in high peaks and low plunges of prosperity and depression, high prices and "no market," feverish employment and long stretches of intermittent work, which for hundreds of thousands of miners meant no work at all, and for many operators meant bankruptcy. The level of government in the industry was in all essential respects the level of hunting tribes.

During the early days of the industry, the miners, like American manual workers in general, were under the popular illusion that democracy meant the passing of a permanent working class. With the Declaration of Independence the old social stratification of feudal Europe had been wiped out forever. There was plenty of room at the top. Everybody might with perseverance and thrift get to the top. This illusion took on considerable substance from the fact that when the industrial revolution first invaded the coal fields America still offered great tracts of unoccupied lands to satisfy the universal land hunger, whereas in England, for example, the policy of enclosure barred poor men from such untilled land as there was. This circumstance accounts for the slow and erratic development of group organization among American miners as compared with the English. There were many cases like that of the bituminous miners in Maryland, who went into the mines; took wages and working conditions as they found them; organized; fought for better wages and working conditions; accumulated a little money; and then, instead of using it to build a permanent organization, broke away for the free lands of the West.

"Their ambition in life," writes Andrew Roy, himself at the time a miner, "was to save enough money to buy a farm in Iowa or Wisconsin. They would go back to the mines in the autumn after harvesting, work all winter, and return with their fresh stake in the spring. None of them ever returned permanently to the mines."

But as the fertile lands were preempted and America became increasingly a manufacturing nation, the coal industry acquired a measure of stability and drew into the mining communities an increasing body of men for whom mining was to be a life's work. The condition of life for these permanent miners was largely determined by the camps or villages which the companies built at the mines. These were generally mean, cheap, temporary affairs. For the faster the miner works, the faster he skims the cream, leaving the more inaccessible coal to waste where it lies, the greater the profit, the better the wages, and the sooner the mine is worked out and abandoned. This, and the caprice of the market in its effect upon the overexpanded industry, meant that the miner must live in his knapsack always prepared to move; and it meant cheap homes and a mean domestic equipment, houses or shacks that might be abandoned without serious loss. To this day the great majority of mining villages have the worst characteristics of city slums intensified by the isolation and loneliness of the country, once beautiful, but now stripped of its forests, its streams running black with the sulphurous waste of the mines. Such moderately attractive cities as Scranton, Wilkes-Barre, and Hazleton in the anthracite region are exceptional. The mining towns that sprawl between Scranton and Wilkes-Barre, or that follow the Panther Creek Valley, are incredibly hideous things. And what is true of the compact and peculiarly prosperous anthracite region is even more true of the sprawling bituminous fields.

The isolation and transitory character of the mining towns made the miners almost completely dependent upon the owners of the mines not only for homes but also for tools and powder; all their mining, as well as their household, supplies. To this day in the non-union fields of West Virginia the operators finance and control, not only the stores, but the schools, the hospitals, the doctors, the churches, and the police. Independent merchants were slow to invest their fortunes in such difficult ground, and since the company store was a convenient means of supplementing the profit from the mines, independent merchants were not encouraged to compete. These conditions tended on the one hand to breed arbitrary management,—autocracy sometimes benevolent, sometimes tyrannical,—and on the other, restlessness, discontent, and the spirit of individual and organized revolt. It set the consciousness of kind in action among the miners especially, and resulted in innumerable local lockouts and strikes.

A sequence of such local struggles occurred in the Blossburg district of Pennsylvania in the '60's and '70's. The Civil War created an abnormal demand for coal, and sent up the price as well as the cost of living generally. In 1863 the miners of the district organized and succeeded in raising their wage rate from thirty-five cents to a dollar and ten cents a ton. At the end of the war, the market broke and the coal fields were flooded with returning soldiers. To protect the standard of living to which during the war they had attained, the miners decided upon a defensive offensive and demanded a further increase of fifteen cents a ton. The operators insisted upon the liquidation of labor. A strike followed. The owners ordered the miners to vacate their company houses. They refused. The local courts issued writs of eviction. To avoid a clash with the sheriff and his deputies, the miners made a holiday in the hills, leaving their hearthstones to their wives. By passive resistance and otherwise, the women held their castles. Then the operators appealed to the governor who sent in the famous Bucktail regiment just victoriously back from the war. They put the miners, their families, and their household goods on the street. The strike was broken. Such miners as were not deported or blacklisted were compelled to accept the terms that were offered, including a pledge to abandon and keep out of their union. So the pendulum swung in 1865.

In 1873 the swing was reversed. Most of the mine owners of Blossburg were also either bankers or retail merchants through their company stores. They were hard hit by the panic of 1873. Without consultation or warning they announced an arbitrary reduction in wages and deferred payment of wages already due. In November they posted notices that the miners might get such goods as they absolutely needed at the company stores, but that no wages would be paid until the following April. Then the miners again drew together in a union. The operators organized in opposition. A lockout strike followed. Strike breakers were brought in, principally a group of recent Swedish immigrants, and marched to a barracks especially prepared for them.

"The strikers gathered on the public highway in front of the barracks," says Andrew Roy, "and insisted on the right to talk with the strikebreakers through one of their interpreters. The managers declined to allow this to be done. But finally a Swedish miner got in among them, and within an hour, the whole of the imported men marched out upon the highway and joined the strikers. The strangers were formed into line, with a Scotch piper at their head, who marched them out of town to the stirring tune of the McGregors' Gathering."

Prevailing public opinion in the '70's, like the prevailing judicial interpretation of the law, frowned upon concerted action by the workers as having the nature of a conspiracy much as the concerted action of the commoners in monarchical days was frowned upon as conspiracy. But curious sorts of circumstances have occasionally arisen to modify opinion in one case as in the other. The Boston Tea Party is our historical example in the political realm. In Blossburg, before this strike of 1873, the miners had been compelled to take their pay in company scrip. Except at the company store, this scrip was worth only from seventy to ninety cents on the dollar.

"When farmers came into mining towns," writes Andrew Roy out of his own experience, "prospective purchasers of their produce would ask them, 'Will you take scrip?' And if the answer was in the affirmative, a dicker would immediately be entered into as to the amount of discount to be allowed."

Independent merchants had gradually ventured into Blossburg. To them the scrip was a competitive injury. When the operators limited the miners to credit at the company stores, the independent merchants protested to the Treasury Department of the United States that the compulsory circulation of company scrip was an illegal infringement of a governmental function. The governor of Pennsylvania took alarm at this appeal over his head and sent the State Secretary of Internal Affairs to investigate. He made a report condemning the operators' practice. The attendant publicity scandalized public opinion and turned it to the miners' side. This time the strike was won.

So by ebb and flow of the consciousness of kind, the elements of a governing structure, the balance of forces between the operators and the miners, gradually formed within the industry. But in the main the balance was determined by public opinion; and public opinion, like the law, was by inherited tradition upon the side of the owners, the accepted custodians of property and the national wealth. Episodes like the use of company scrip tended to even the balance. And more important still in their effect upon the traditional hostility of public opinion toward the unions in their infringement upon the vested rights and privileges of the owners were the great mine disasters.

Some of our coal crops out at the surface in places where through the ages wind and weather have worn away the overlying clay, stone, and slate. This can be gathered like wood in the forest without danger. The amount of such coal is commercially unimportant. Some lies only a few feet underground so that it is possible to take it by stripping away the thin overlying material and blast and scoop it out with a steam shovel. There are some stripping mines in the anthracite field and a considerable number in the alluvial plains of the West. But the great bulk of our coal is reached by driving drifts or headings into the veins through the sides of hills or by sinking shafts scores, or hundreds, or thousands of feet down through the earth to where the coal lies. From the mouth of the drift or the foot of the shaft, a tunnel or main heading or gangway is driven on and on into the coal usually for miles, with secondary tunnels giving off the main heading into the pitch-black rooms where the miners work. In the cryptlike terminal rooms, the miner with his buddy undercuts the "face" of the coal with his pick or with an undercutting machine, drills shot-holes into the face, sets his charge of powder and tamps it in, and then shoots the coal down. Sometimes, for the sake of speed, he shoots it down without undercutting, and in the anthracite mines where the coal is too hard for undercutting, direct shooting from the face is the general practice. This blasting of a friable and inflammable substance fills the cellared air with minute particles of highly explosive dust. As the mines go deeper and further away from the opening they accumulate gas and underground water. The greatest number of injuries and deaths in the mines, and coal mining is among the most hazardous of all occupations, result from the falling of overhanging rock and coal; but the catastrophies which have shocked public opinion into a sympathetic attitude toward the commoners of the mines do not come from this steady death toll but have resulted from explosions or fires that have trapped and suffocated or burned their scores and hundreds.

It seems incredible, in view of the known hazards of underground work, that there should ever have been opposition to the installation of all available safeguards. But it must be remembered that we are still very close to primitive man, that the consciousness of kind and the instinct of brotherhood are still hard pressed by the primal acquisitive instinct. In America in spite of potential plenty the community's first preoccupation was escape from hunger, the winning of individual and national economic security. The prevailing attitude toward death and injury in the mines was, and to a great extent still is, much the same as the prevailing attitude toward death and injury in battle. In ordinary days of peace we do not glorify the soldier. Similarly, it is only at time of disaster that our sympathetic understanding goes out to the shock troops in our war against nature, the men who with pick and powder win coal underground.

"So numerous and heartrending," says Roy, "had these accidents become (in the anthracite field) that the miners of Schuylkill county in the year 1858 appealed to the legislature for the passage of a law to provide for official supervision of the mines, and a bill for the purpose was introduced the same year; but it found no countenance, and never came to a vote. In 1866 it was again introduced, and passed the lower house, but it was defeated in the Senate. In 1869 it was reintroduced, passed both houses and received the approval of the governor of the state. It provided for *one* mine inspector for Schuylkill county, *the other counties being left out.* The law had been in operation only a few months when the Avondale shaft in the adjoining county of Luzerne took fire and suffocated every soul in the mine including two daring miners who went down the mine after the fire, in the hope of rescuing some of the entombed men. The shaft had but one opening.... The whole underground force of the mine, 109 souls, were suffocated to death by the gases emanating from the burning woodwork in the shaft and the breakers on top of it.... No catastrophe ever occurred in this country which created a greater sensation than this mining horror. The public press united in demanding the passage of all laws necessary for the protection of the health and lives of the miners.... When the legislature met in the following January a committee of representative miners was sent to Harrisburg to have a mining bill enacted into law for the proper security of the lives, health, and safety of the anthracite miners of Pennsylvania, which was promptly done."

Stirred by the Avondale disaster, the miners of the Mahoning Valley in Ohio had a bill introduced into the Ohio legislature calling for two separate openings in all mines employing more than ten men underground, for the forced circulation to the face of the coal of at least one hundred cubic feet of air per minute for each underground worker, the daily inspection of all gaseous mines by a fireviewer before the miners were allowed to enter, the appointment of four state mine inspectors, and the right of the miners to appoint a check-weighman at their own expense to see that their coal was fairly weighed at the tipple. As soon as the bill was printed, a committee of thirteen operators representing every mining district in the state, supported by legal counsel and the state geologist, appeared in opposition. Their contention was that the miners of the state did not want the law, that the bill was the invention of professional demagogues and labor agitators who sponged a fat living off the ignorance and cupidity of their misguided followers, that there was neither gas nor bad air in Ohio mines, that the lives and fortunes of the miners were safe in the hands of their employers, that the bill was special legislation and unconstitutional and that if enacted by the General Assembly of Ohio it would be set aside by the Supreme Court. The bill was defeated, but a commission of inquiry was appointed. At the next session of the General Assembly the miners' bill was reintroduced and passed by a unanimous vote. But before it was sent to the governor, the operators again sent a committee to defeat it. It was amended and all provision for state inspection of the mines stricken out. In the following June a disaster occurred in a mine in Portage county owned by the member of the legislature who had emasculated the bill. This mine, too, had but one opening which an accidental fire converted into a furnace. There were twenty-one men in the mine. Ten were burned to death and the eleven who managed to escape through the smoke and flame were terribly injured. The miners' bill was reintroduced and again opposed. Judge Hoadly, afterwards governor of Ohio, speaking in opposition very accurately expressed the prevailing state of mind. "We have tried to make men sober and moral by law," he said, "and now we are going to try to surround them with protection against carelessness and danger, and enable them to shut their eyes and walk in darkness, satisfied with the care and protection of the state. I admit that there is a line to which the right of the legislature—the duty of the legislature—may go without infringing on the natural right of the citizen; but what I want to suggest as the safe side, is to leave the people free, and to allow mishap and disaster to have its natural effect as the penalty for and the cure of the evils which result from negligence which causes mishap and disaster." But in spite of this persuasive reasoning, the miners' bill, after years of effort, was finally enacted into law.

Thus slowly the consciousness of kind worked through the public to the miners, under the influence of such understanding as mining catastrophies shocked into the public mind. But the main force that made for the improvement of their conditions of work, for the development of standards of living among them and of orderly processes of government within the industry as a whole was the operation of the consciousness of kind within their own group.

The processes of civilization like all cosmic processes are slow. The period of recorded history is but a minute in the unnumbered years of man's life upon earth. It was by slow stages that the blind herd instinct which sends wolves hunting in packs and leads birds to migrate in flocks merged into the consciousness of kind and the spirit of service among men. So in the coal industry, the miners organized slowly, first in local groups, then by districts, then on a national scale with the beginnings of international affiliations. They drew together into unions, broke apart, drew together again. As they acquired strength, their interests came into conflict with the interests of the coal owners. There were strikes and lockouts, local joint agreements, then strikes and lockouts again, then other agreements for arbitration and conciliation, then more strikes and lockouts. That process still goes on as in the bitter civil war in West Virginia. But in the main it reached a culmination so far as the coal industry is concerned when in 1902 President Roosevelt intervened in the interests of the consumers, asserted a balance of power between and over the two groups, and established the foundations of orderly government within the industry. The processes by which representative government has grown up within the industry run closely parallel with the processes by which the parliamentary government arose in the European political states, with property owners performing the very important function of technical organization and development which in the early stages of national life the monarch and his executives performed, and the miners playing the rôle of the commoners. It is upon this historical structure that the future of the industry as a public service depends.

CHAPTER VI
THE STRUGGLE FOR ORGANIZATION

In their volume on The Church and Industrial Reconstruction, the Committee on the War and the Religious Outlook, an interdenominational group appointed by the joint action of the Federal Council of Churches and the General Wartime Commission of the Churches, declare that "Democracy is the attempt to realize this fundamental right of every personality to self-expression through cooperation with others in a common task. In the political sphere it has already found large recognition.... It applies, or should apply, in the sphere of organized religion, which is the Church. It applies in the sphere of industry. Indeed, it may be of relatively small significance for men to have the right of political self-expression, unless they have similar opportunity for self-expression in their daily work. For the conditions which affect them in industry touch them more closely than the concerns of the state."

It is for this reason that the study of the growth of democratic organization and government in industry inevitably stresses the growth of organization and orderly processes among the workers, the commoners of industry. The political revolution of the eighteenth century emancipated the owners of property from the autocratic control of the monarchical state. But, as Sidney and Beatrice Webb have pointed out, "the framers of the United States Constitution, like the various parties in the French Revolution of 1789, saw no resemblance or analogy between the personal power which they drove from the castle, the altar, and the throne, and that which they left unchecked in the farm, the factory, and the mine. Even at the present day, after a century of revolution, the great mass of middle- and upper-class 'Liberals' all over the world see no more inconsistency between democracy and unrestrained capitalist enterprise, than Washington and Jefferson did between democracy and slave-owning. The 'dim, inarticulate' multitude of manual-working wage-earners have, from the outset, felt their way to a different view. To them, the uncontrolled power wielded by the owners of the means of production, able to withhold from the manual worker all chance of subsistence unless he accepted their terms, meant a far more genuine loss of liberty, and a far keener sense of personal subjection, than the official jurisdiction of the magistrate, or the far-off, impalpable rule of the king. The captains of industry, like the kings of yore, are honestly unable to understand why their personal power should be interfered with.... The agitation for freedom of combination and factory legislation has been, in reality, a demand for a 'constitution' in the industrial realm."

What the Committee on the War and the Religious Outlook and the Webbs state in slightly different language explains why the history of constitutional government in industry is fundamentally the history of the rise of the workers through their unions and collective bargaining toward a democratic equality of status with their employers.

As soon as the mining communities became sufficiently stable to allow the consciousness of kind to operate, the miners began to organize into small local groups for mutual aid, to care for one another in sickness, to bury one another at death, and to improve their wages and working conditions. But it was not until after the industrial revolution got under full headway during and immediately after the Civil War that they became actively conscious of a community of interest over wide areas. For the structure of modern democratic government in industry as in nations and among nations, depends upon railroads, the postal and telegraph service, and other means of communication. A strong impetus and a definite direction was given to the existing tendency toward organization by the steady infiltration of miners from Great Britain where constitutional government in the coal industry had already made considerable progress and where the miners were firmly organized. The miners held their first national convention in St. Louis, Missouri, in January, 1861. The call had been issued by Daniel Weaver, an English trade-unionist, who after the failure of the Chartist movement had settled in the coal fields of Illinois.

"The necessity of an association of miners and of those branches of industry immediately connected with mining operations, having for its object the physical, mental, and social elevation of the miner, has long been felt by the thinking portion of the miners generally," said Weaver in his call. "Union is the great fundamental principle by which every object of importance is to be accomplished. Man is a social being and if left to himself in an isolated condition is one of the weakest of creatures, but when associated with his kind he works wonders.... There is an electric sympathy kindled, the attractive forces inherent in human nature are called into action and a stream of generous emotion binds together and animates the whole.... Our unity is essential to the attainment of our rights and the amelioration of our present condition.... Our safety, our remedy, our protection, our dearest interests, and the social well-being of our families, present and future, depend upon our unity, our duty, and our regard for each other."

The convention formed the American Miners' Association, elected Weaver secretary and Thomas Lloyd, another English immigrant, president. A considerable number of miners in Illinois, Indiana, Ohio, Pennsylvania, and Maryland joined the union, which exerted a mild influence upon the legislatures of the several states. But the Association was a national organization in name only. The miners had not yet learned to work together under the direction of their own leaders. The organization was not strong enough to withstand the break in the labor market and the anti-union drive that attended the flood of returning soldiers at the end of the Civil War. Moreover, the American public regarded the trade union as an alien institution, the evil creation of "foreigners" and alien "agitators." It was held to be contrary to the genius of American life that workers should combine to interfere with the sanctity of property and the prerogatives that inhered in that sanctity just as it had been so held in England a century before. Even by the great majority of wage workers as by the public at large the accepted theory, carried over from the feudal tradition of Europe, was that the rights and interests of both would be best protected and cared for "by the Christian men to whom God has given control of the property interests of the country."

Under stress of the panic of 1873, and after a series of unsuccessful strikes to maintain wages, the American Miners' Association went to pieces. But local unions, generally known as "Miners' and Laborers' Benevolent Associations," kept up a struggling existence. The strongest of these was the Workingmen's Benevolent Association, a consolidation of all the local unions in the anthracite field. It was largely the creation of John Siney, an Englishbred Irishman, among the keenest minds the labor movement has produced. One of the first acts of this Benevolent Association was to declare a suspension of work in order to relieve the mines of the glut of coal which had resulted from the slack industrial period following the Civil War. This maneuver met with condemnation of the press and from the operators, who did not, nevertheless, regard it with entire disfavor, since it had a considerable effect in maintaining prices as well as wages. As soon as the suspension had accomplished its purpose the miners returned to work, and immediately thereafter John Siney succeeded in persuading the anthracite owners to enter a conference with representatives of the union. The first joint meeting of operators and miners was held in Scranton in 1869, and as a result of this conference the first joint agreement ever made between American miners and operators for the establishment of a wage scale was signed on July 29, 1870, by five members of the Anthracite Board of Trade and five representatives of the Workingmen's Benevolent Association.

This unique achievement made Siney a national figure. Local leaders in all parts of the country appealed to him to call another national convention. On his initiative, the Miners' National Association was constituted by the convention held in Youngstown, Ohio, in October, 1873. The convention elected Siney president. National headquarters were opened in Cleveland.

Wearied with endless strikes the convention had made arbitration, conciliation, and cooperation the basic principles of their constitution. Fortified with these principles, Siney and an associate visited the offices of all the coal companies in Cleveland. All except one of the operators turned them down. They would have nothing to do with a union. The exception was Marcus A. Hanna. When Siney assured Hanna that no strike would be called without previous resort to arbitration and that the officers of the union would order the men to keep at work even if an award went against them, Hanna accepted their proposition and undertook to bring the other operators into line. In spite of the widespread depression in the coal trade the National Association grew rapidly. Twenty-one thousand members were represented at the second convention held in Cleveland in October, 1874. But notwithstanding Hanna's great influence, many of the operators remained hostile to the union. Toward the close of 1874, the operators of the Tuscarawas Valley in Ohio announced a wage cut from ninety to seventy cents a ton. The miners determined to strike. Siney induced them to resort to arbitration. The umpire admitted a reduction to seventy-one cents. The miners were bitter against the decision which had gone almost completely against them. Only the great influence of Siney restrained them from striking at once.

Then one of the operators, the Crawford Coal Company, took advantage of the discontent. This company had refused to join Hanna and his associates in dealing with the union. During the arbitration proceedings, the Crawford Company locked out their men for demanding a check-weighman, and appealed to the operators' association for support. The associated operators refused. The Crawford Company then offered their locked-out men an advance of nine cents a ton above the rate fixed for the union miners by the arbitration award. The acquisitive instinct was stronger than the consciousness of kind among the non-union miners. They accepted and went back to work.

This turn of the wheel broke Siney's control over the organization. His followers threatened to desert unless he repudiated the arbitration award. He refused. But his executive board, in a desperate effort to save the union, overruled him and yielded. Strikes and lockouts followed in quick succession. Hanna was as helpless as Siney. Strike breakers were imported, under cover men and troops were brought in. Arbitration, constitutional government, and the union went on the rocks.

Similar misfortune attended Siney's pioneer efforts to establish the union and constitutional government in his home district at Clearfield, Pennsylvania. No sooner had the miners joined the National Association than they expected Siney and his fellow executives to achieve quick redress of their grievances and to force an advance in wages. They grew impatient with the slow processes of negotiation. They struck against the advice of Siney. Immediately the operators in the Clearfield district followed the precedent of Tuscarawas. They brought in strike breakers and troops. A brief civil war followed. Some heads were broken. The strike was lost. In spite of his heroic efforts to keep the peace and to establish orderly processes of government, Siney was arrested for conspiracy and thrown into jail. The morale of the Miners' National Association was broken, and like its predecessors it went by the board.

Like the tides of the sea, the consciousness of kind ebbed and flowed among the miners. They drew together into local, state, and national organizations, held for brief periods, and then scattered again under the impact of the operators supported by prevailing public opinion. They had not become fully group conscious; neither had the public come to recognize their unions as essential arms of constitutional government within the industry.

In the bounteous days of national expansion, in the exuberant '70's and '80's, a vague belief was abroad that America would never develop a permanent working class. Every man was "as good as" another, and the hustling, self-made business man was the American ideal. In accord with this theory was one of the significant actions of the Miners' National Association, an attempt to buy coal lands to be operated by the miners, not as a workers' cooperative association, but as a corporation of business men. During the '70's and the '80's also the Knights of Labor built up a great following among the wage-workers, largely on the philosophy that if they kept free of "class-conscious" trade unions and went in for a mass movement of all workers, they could by some strange alchemy of the American spirit rise to the status of independent business men. The Knights of Labor played much the same rôle among the wage-workers that the various "populist" movements played among the farmers before the development of such group-conscious tendencies as those which in our day have developed the farmers' cooperative societies and the agricultural bloc.

The labor movement as we know it today in America began when in 1886 Samuel Gompers became first president of the American Federation of Labor, an office which with the interruption of a single year he has held ever since. Mr. Gompers led the wage-workers to a frank acceptance of the prevailing business and acquisitive ideals as the basis, not of individual escape from the working class, but of their consolidation into trade unions for the businesslike control and sale of their craft skill through collective bargaining. It is significant that the immediate precursor of the American Federation of Labor—the Organized Trades Unions of the United States of America and Canada, over whose councils Mr. Gompers exercised great influence—demanded the legal incorporation of trade unions and a protective tariff for American labor, as well as the prohibition of child labor under fourteen, the eight-hour day, the abolition of conspiracy laws, and the other reforms which constitute the present program of organized labor. By the frank recognition of the basic force of the acquisitive instinct in human nature, the realistic leaders of the new labor movement were able to release and consolidate the consciousness of kind for effective operation within the wage-working group.

The influence of this new philosophy made itself felt throughout all the skilled trades and notably among the miners. After the break-up of the Miners' National Association, the miners maintained state organizations in Ohio, Illinois, Pennsylvania, and in several other states. They steadily took the initiative in seeking conferences and negotiations with the operators of their districts. In spite of the failure of arbitration under the pioneering leadership of Siney, they supported the agitation which resulted in the Trade Tribunal Act of Pennsylvania (1883), and the similar arbitration act of Ohio (1885).

But the process of overdevelopment which has always characterized the American coal industry created sharp fluctuations of prosperity and market depression and afforded an unstable basis for the establishment of the machinery of orderly government. Both miners and operators showed a tendency to run wild. Conferences were held, arbitration agreements occasionally entered into, but now one side, now the other, repudiated the awards as the fluctuating market sent prices erratically up and down. The needs of the community have always called for the integration of the industry, but the happy-go-lucky American spirit persistently shied away from public regulation as long as the acquisitive instinct could be satisfied at however great a cost in profligate use and waste. But this very overdevelopment, with its destructive effect upon wages and regularity of employment, continually brought the miners back to a consciousness of the need for national organization.

In 1885, John McBride, president of the Ohio Miners' State Union, and later, for a single term, president of the American Federation of Labor, issued a call to the miners of the United States to meet in convention on the ninth of September in Indianapolis. Seven states sent delegates. The National Federation of Miners and Mine Laborers was formed and its Executive Board issued a call *to the mine operators of the United States and territories* inviting them to a joint meeting for the purpose of adjusting market and mining prices in such a way as to avoid strikes and lockouts, and to give to each party an increased profit from the sale of coal. Only one operator, Mr. W. P. Rend of Chicago, paid any attention to this call. He inspired the miners to persevere. They sent out a second invitation. A dozen or so operators met with the executive board in Chicago and agreed upon a joint call for a national joint convention to be held in Pittsburgh in December.

"The undersigned committee," the invitation said, "consisting of three mine owners, and three delegates representing the miners' organization, were appointed to make a general public presentation of the objects and purposes of this convention, and to extend an invitation to all those engaged in coal mining in America, to lend their active cooperation toward the establishment of harmony and friendship between capital and labor in this large and important industry.... Apart and in conflict capital and labor become agents of evil, while united they create blessings of plenty and prosperity.... Capital represents the accumulation, or savings, of past labor, while labor is the most sacred part of capital.... It is evident that the general standard of reward for labor has sunk too low.... It is equally true that the widespread depression of business, the overproduction of coal, and the consequent severe competition have caused the capital invested in mines to yield little or no profitable returns. The constant reductions of wages that have lately taken place have afforded no relief to capital, and, indeed, have tended to increase its embarrassments.... This is the first movement of a national character in America, taken with the intention of the establishment of labor conciliation...."

In response to this call a small joint meeting was held in Pittsburgh in December. It adjourned for a second conference in Columbus, Ohio, in February, 1886. Here the operators were represented by seventy-seven delegates, principally from Ohio, but also from Pennsylvania, Indiana, Illinois, Maryland, and West Virginia. They adopted a national wage scale, established a national board of arbitration, and provided for the creation of similar state boards to maintain industrial peace and to develop the structure and processes of constitutional government.

The agreement held and worked in spite of the opposition of groups of operators, notably in the West Virginia field and the steel district of Pittsburgh, and the individualistic lethargy of many of the miners. The new philosophy of business trade unionism gripped the miners, made the trade union policy triumphant over the vaguely utopian policy of the Knights of Labor, and resulted in the consolidation of the miners' organizations into the United Mine Workers of America in 1890. But the process of overdevelopment continued in the industry. The workings of the joint machinery creaked and faltered under the impact of strikes and lockouts due in the main to market fluctuations, and for a decade the United Mine Workers, in spite of periods of prosperity and rapid growth, was perpetually threatened with the fate of its predecessors.

This fate was averted by the economic developments which had converted the compact anthracite field into a virtual monopoly under the combined control of the anthracite railroads and the great banking houses of the East that owned the railroads. While the bituminous industry sprawled and overdeveloped, the anthracite combination gradually restricted the production of anthracite to the calculable demand of the market. This made for stability in the anthracite field, which is reflected in the fact that while even today the average working year in the bituminous fields is approximately two hundred and fifteen days,—an average working day when spread over the year, of less than four hours,—the working year in the anthracite field gradually rose until today it holds steady at something more than two hundred and sixty days a year.

This stability enabled the anthracite miners to accumulate an economic surplus above their immediate needs and set the consciousness of kind in vigorous operation among them. By 1900 they had developed the nucleus of a strong organization. Their wages, however, had lagged behind the wages of the miners in the better-organized bituminous fields. On their demand, the national officers of the United Mine Workers called a convention of anthracite representatives in Hazleton, Pennsylvania, "to devise means by which a joint convention of operators and miners can be held" to consider the upward readjustment of the anthracite wage scale and "methods to abolish the pernicious system now in vogue in the anthracite region by which a part of the earnings of the mine workers is taken from them by the infamous system of dockage, and by the practice of compelling mine workers to load more than 2240 pounds for a ton." The operators disregarded the convention's invitation to a joint conference. The men struck. The operators made concessions but refused to deal with the union. The men accepted the concessions and returned to work. During the next two years they fortified their treasury and prepared to strike again. John Mitchell had become president of the United Mine Workers. In February, 1902, he addressed a circular letter to the presidents of the anthracite railroads inviting them to a joint conference. The railroad presidents refused to have anything to do with the union. The anthracite miners then made a public proposal that the issues should be submitted to the arbitration of the Industrial Branch of the National Civic Federation, of which Senator Hanna was chairman, or of Archbishop Ireland, Bishop Potter, and one other person to be selected by these two. But all such tentatives were also rejected by the operators. It was about this time that Mr. George F. Baer, president of the Philadelphia and Reading Coal Company and of the Reading Railway System, made his interesting declaration that "the rights and interests of the laboring man will be protected and cared for, not by the labor agitators, but by the Christian men to whom God has given the control of the property interests of the country."

Efforts at conference and arbitration having failed, the anthracite miners called a strike. Only a minority of the men had previously joined the union, but ninety men in a hundred obeyed the strike call. The bituminous miners were eager to declare a sympathetic strike, but they had collective agreements in the more important fields and their president, John Mitchell, and their secretary, William

B. Wilson, afterwards Secretary of Labor in President Wilson's cabinet, insisted upon honoring these contracts. Trade union discipline had grown stronger since the days of Siney and Mitchell's counsel prevailed. The anthracite strike dragged on throughout the summer. Winter was approaching. President Roosevelt decided to intervene. There was no precedent for such intervention in the coal industry, which though basic to the industrial life of the nation, was held sacred to the traditional rights of private ownership and business initiative. In his address to the miners and operators, President Roosevelt expressed his sense of the unprecedented character of his action.

"As long," he said, "as there seemed to be a reasonable hope that these matters could be adjusted between the parties it did not seem proper for me to interfere in any way. I disclaim any right or duty to interfere in any way, upon legal grounds or upon any official relation that I bear to the situation. But the urgency and the terrible nature of the catastrophe impending, where a large portion of our people, in the shape of a winter fuel famine, are concerned, impel me after anxious thought to believe that my duty requires me to use whatever influence I personally can bring to bear to end a situation which has become literally impossible."

In spite of his disavowal of legal authority or official responsibility, President Roosevelt's action was publicly regarded as the official action of the nation's chief executive. It gave the public its first intimation of the status of coal as that of a public utility. It stamped upon the coal industry the character of an essential public service which has attached to it ever since. Backed by public opinion, which would have sustained him if he had declared the existence of a public emergency and had taken over the anthracite industry as the government did the entire coal industry during the war, he was able to force the submission of the dispute to a commission of arbitration by whose decision both sides pledged themselves to abide. The strike was settled. A machinery of government was established and put into operation. As the result of President Roosevelt's action, collective bargaining was for the first time given public sanction not only in the anthracite field but throughout the coal industry. For seventeen years, and indeed, with the exception of a brief interval in 1919, for twenty years, peace and constitutional government prevailed not only in the anthracite field, but, with the exception of a few districts, notably certain counties in West Virginia and the coking fields subsidiary to the steel industry in Pennsylvania, Colorado, and Alabama, throughout the bituminous fields also.

The structure of this government and its basic laws are written into collective contracts, which, together with the policies formulated by the two parties through their national organizations, must be our guides in the quest for an answer to the question as to how, short of the autocratic control of the Fuel Administration, the coal industry is to be developed into an integrated, dependably governed, public service.

CHAPTER VII
THE RISE OF DEMOCRACY

The historians of the growth of democratic government in the coal industry generally date the establishment of collective bargaining as a permanent institution from 1898, when the operators of the Central Competitive Field—Western Pennsylvania, Ohio, Indiana, and Illinois—in a joint conference with the representatives of the United Mine Workers of America entered into an agreement which with minor modifications was periodically renewed from that time onward. From that year to 1922 operators and miners alike recognized the agreement in the Central Competitive Field as basic to the agreements in all other fields and the central competitive conference as the necessary prelude to all other conferences. But it was President Roosevelt and the Anthracite Strike Commission which he appointed that lifted human relationships within the industry out of the limbo of frontier strife and periodic guerrilla warfare and stamped them with the quasi-public character of a self-governing constitutional democracy.

From the beginning, certain of the coal owners, notably those in sections of West Virginia and Alabama, whose coking coals make them economically subsidiary to the steel industry, have held strongly to the autocratic powers and privileges which the conception of property carried over from the pre-revolutionary monarchical days when the king was generally recognized, *Dei gratia*, as the custodian of the national hoard. But the Roosevelt Commission took the stand which has increasingly won public acceptance, that autocracy in industry is incompatible with democracy in the political state, and that they must both rise or fall together. Forms may change, but it may be taken as axiomatic that if democracy is the law determining the evolution of political civilization,—if it is the condition of the full development of the individual personality and the attainment of the good life and human brotherhood,—it will survive and grow in industry as well as in the political realm. It is from this principle of democratic evolution, and not from the strikes and lock-outs and barterings over wages, hours, and profits incidental to its development, that collective bargaining and industrial democracy derive their fundamental significance.

In appointing the Commission "at the request both of the operators and of the miners," President Roosevelt asked them not only to pass upon the questions in controversy, but also "to establish the relations between the employers and the wage workers in the anthracite fields on a just and permanent basis."

In arbitrating the immediate questions in dispute,—questions of wages, hours, and working conditions,—the Commission, even after months of hearings at which hundreds of witnesses appeared, found themselves in the usual predicament of arbitrators and the lay public in such circumstances. The facts about the industry,—its capital investment, its financial organization, its earnings and profits, the cost of living in the district, the organization of work in the mines, the character of the work, the skill which it required, and its attendant hazards,—had never been scientifically determined. Then as now these essential facts were held to lie within the sacred province of private business enterprise and not within the legitimate scope of public inquiry and revelation. In instance after instance, they found that statistics of the kind presented were "rather too inexact for a satisfactory basis on which to make precise calculations." On the demands of the miners and the counter-demands of the operators, they were reluctantly constrained to adopt the usual refuge of arbitration tribunals set up in an emergency; they "split the difference." The miners, for example, asked for a twenty per cent increase in their rate of wages; the Commission granted them ten per cent. Other issues were not susceptible of such definite arbitrament, but in general the Commission, striving to hold the scales of justice even, followed the rule of fifty-fifty.

In presenting their award, the Commission, keenly aware of the almost impossible burden which the absence of scientific knowledge with respect to this basic industry placed upon them, declared that "all through their investigations and deliberations the conviction had grown upon them that if they could evoke and confirm a more genuine spirit of good will, a more conciliatory disposition in the operators and their employes in their relations toward one another, they would do a better and more lasting work than any which mere rulings, however wise and just, may accomplish." It was with this end in view that they set up a scheme of constitutional democratic government within the industry.

Quotation is often dull, but nothing can take the place of direct quotation in the case of a document of epoch-making importance. By way of justifying their action the Commission declared that "in the days when the employer had but a few employes, personal acquaintance and direct contact of the employer and employe resulted in mutual knowledge of the surrounding conditions and the desires of each. The development of the employers into large corporations has rendered such personal contact and acquaintance between the responsible employer and the individual employe no longer possible in the old sense. The tendency toward peace and good-fellowship which flows out of personal acquaintance or direct contact should not, however, be lost through this evolution of great combinations. There seems to be no medium through which to preserve it, so natural and efficient as that of an organization of employes governed by rules which represent the will of a properly constituted majority of its members, and officered by members selected for that purpose, and in whom authority to administer the rules and affairs of the union and its members is vested."

The anthracite operators had conditioned their submission to the award of the Commission by refusing to be drawn into a collective agreement with the miners' national organization, the United Mine Workers of America. The Commission got around this technicality by constituting the anthracite district divisions of the union and the organized anthracite operators the two houses of the anthracite parliament. The democratic government which they set up is typical of the scheme of government which now prevails through eighty per cent of the coal industry, and which, while it is subject to the fluctuations characteristic of all democratic institutions, may be taken as permanent in principle.

Again, because of its historical importance, the language of the Commission calls for direct quotation. The Commission decreed: "That any difficulty or disagreement arising under this award, either as to interpretation or application, or in any way growing out of the relations of the employers and employed, which can not be settled or adjusted by consultation between the superintendent or manager of the mine or mines and the miner or miners directly interested, or is of a scope too large to be so settled or adjusted, shall be referred to a permanent joint committee, to be called a board of conciliation, to consist of six persons, appointed as hereinafter provided. That is to say, if there shall be a division of the whole region into three districts, in each of which there shall exist an organization representing a majority of the mine workers of such district, one of said board of conciliation shall be appointed by each of said organizations, and three persons shall be appointed by the operators, the operators in each of said districts appointing one person.

"The board of conciliation thus constituted shall take up and consider any question referred to it as aforesaid, hearing both parties to the controversy, and such evidence as may be laid before it by either party; and any award made by a majority of such board of conciliation shall be final and binding on all parties. If, however, the said board is unable to decide any question submitted, or point related thereto, that question or point shall be referred to an umpire, to be appointed, at the request of said board, by one of the circuit judges of the third judicial circuit of the United States, whose decision shall be final and binding in the premises.

"The membership of said board shall at all times be kept complete, either the operators or the miners' organizations having the right, at any time when a controversy is not pending, to change their representation thereon.

"At all hearings before said board the parties may be represented by such person or persons as they may respectively select.

"No suspension of work shall take place, by lock-out or strike, pending the adjudication of any matter so taken up for adjustment."

From the date of the Commission's award to 1919, when President Wilson created a similar commission to avert a threatened break, the anthracite operators and miners, who were invariably represented by the presidents of the three district organizations of the United Mine Workers of America, lived at peace under this constitution.

The machinery of constitutional government thus given public sanction in the anthracite field is in its general outline and provisions typical of the machinery which through joint conference and negotiation the organized miners and operators have worked out throughout the greater part of the bituminous fields. The miners act under the authority of their national convention when it is in session and under the general direction of their national president and executive board, acting under laws devised by the national convention in the interval between the national convention's biennial sessions. Within the limitations set by the national laws of the organization, the four thousand local unions and the twenty-seven district unions exercise a degree of local autonomy analogous to the local autonomy of our cities, towns, counties, and states. In fact the entire national organization is built up from the mine committees at the individual mines, which, conjointly with the representative of the management at the mine, are the courts of original jurisdiction. As in the case of our states in relation to the federal government, these local bodies reserve all authority that is not specifically delegated to the national organization through its constitution and the action of the national convention, the representative national congress of the union. Unlike the President of the United States, the president of the United Mine Workers has no power to appoint and remove his cabinet—the National Executive Board—but through his power over the national organizers and the other agents of the national office, he is in a position to control the political machinery of the organization. By virtue of its form of organization, the miners' union has the virtues as well as the defects of our American political organization, defects which are the price of self-government and the educative processes of self-government.

Because of the compact nature of the anthracite field and its domination by a small group of railroads, the operators of this field have acted in concert for many decades. But until 1917, the coal owners of the country had no national organization. In that year, for the purposes of negotiation with the federal government relative to the controlled production and price of bituminous coal, they organized the National Coal Association. Unlike the miners' national organization, this Association is not by its certificate of incorporation explicitly concerned with the wage contract or industrial relations as such. Its primary object is the "encouragement and fostering of the general welfare of the coal-mining industry" as a business enterprise. It is, however, acquiring many of the functions of the miners' union. In recent controversies it has actively assisted the local operators' associations in their dealings with their organized employes. And like the miners' national organization it actively concerns itself with the protection and advancement of the interests of its members in Congress and the state legislatures. But the immense extent of the bituminous coal fields and the highly competitive character of the industry, which has been artificially maintained by the Sherman law, has prevented the compact organization of the bituminous operators and has limited concerted action, especially in matters affecting the labor contract, almost entirely to local, state, and district associations. It is upon the miners' organization that the operators largely rely to equalize competitive conditions. For wages constitute the largest single item of cost in coal production and it is only through the ability of the miners' union to negotiate on a nation-wide basis that this burden can be equalized for the thousands of competing operators.

The inability of the operators to achieve a national organization has not only contributed to the overdevelopment of the industry with consequences that became critically manifest during the war, but has also greatly complicated the struggle of the miners to establish collective negotiation and agreement on a national scale.

In Illinois, for example, there are three operators' associations which have been organized to deal with labor. The oldest of these is the Illinois Coal Operators' Association formed in 1897. During a wage controversy in 1910 the operators of the fifth and ninth Illinois districts broke away from the parent body and formed an association of their own. In 1914, the operators of the Springfield district organized the independent Central Illinois Coal Operators' Association. Diversity of mining conditions in the various sections of the Illinois coal field and the inability of the operators to equalize competitive costs without the help of the miners were responsible for these secessions. One of the objects enumerated in the constitution of the Central Illinois Coal Operators' Association is "to protect the interest of the members of this association in the making of district, state, and interstate contracts with the United Mine Workers, to the end that such members shall obtain scales, rates, prices, conditions, and *such differentials* from the basic rates as the relative physical and other working conditions of the mines owned by them entitle them to." An identical clause appears in the constitution of the Coal Operators' Association of the fifth and ninth districts of Illinois. In 1910 the operators in these two districts were paying seven cents a ton more than other members of the parent association. They seceded and entered into a separate agreement with the union in the hope that the union would be able to abolish this unfavorable differential. The union succeeded only in reducing the differential to four cents. While these three associations compete with one another for terms with the miners' union within their own state, they cooperate in their common effort to secure from the miners terms that will place them at a competitive advantage as against operators in other states. This rivalry among the operators makes the diplomatic problem of the union's national officers a very difficult one and when groups of operators, like those in certain counties of West Virginia and Alabama, refuse to deal with the union at all and impose cut-rate wage scales upon their unorganized employes as a basis for cutting the price of coal in the limited market, the industry is thrown into confusion bordering upon anarchy. The operators in the organized fields hold the union responsible for its failure to organize the anti-union fields and so to equalize competitive conditions. Many of them decide that their only remedy is to break with the union and through individual bargaining with their employes when the labor market is overstocked force down wages and working conditions to the level of the anti-union fields. The organized miners are thus compelled to fight for their organization and the maintenance of their dearly won standard of living. Strikes and lockouts temporarily take the place of the orderly processes of joint negotiation, conciliation, and collective agreement as in the spring of 1922.

The processes of conflict and cooperation through which government in industry, as in the state, evolves, are as truly cosmic processes as those through which the coal measures themselves were created, with the humanly significant difference that the processes of social evolution are, within certain limits, controllable by the will of man. The policy of democratic peoples and therefore of their governments is to allow the maximum freedom of development to government within industry compatible with the comfort and economic security of the community as a whole. Where the security of the community is threatened, the government tends to intervene as President Roosevelt did in the case of the anthracite controversy. And while the traditional bias of government and the law,—the bias which they inherited from the feudal society which existed when the industrial revolution began,—favors the owners of property to which a special sanctity still adheres, public opinion among peoples devoted to democracy in the political state increasingly tends to assert itself in favor of democracy in industry, and more especially such basic industries as the railroads and coal. It is for this reason that it is logical to assume that the point of view toward collective bargaining, expressed by President Roosevelt's Commission and incorporated into the social creeds of most of the Christian denominations, will ultimately prevail. And since collective bargaining and the orderly processes of government initiated by the joint labor contracts are the historical foundations of democracy in industry, it is also reasonable to infer that collective bargaining will increasingly become the rule in industrial relations.

But there are large issues of momentous public concern which do not come within the scope of collective bargaining. Rule 15 in the standard agreement between the operators and the miners in the bituminous fields of central Pennsylvania specifically forbids the miners to concern themselves in any way with the problems of management and the technical equipment and organization of the mines. Because of the great abundance of coal, the industry had been developed by overexpansion and wasteful skimming rather than by the application of scientific methods to the mining of the best coal and its efficient utilization. Not only is one ton of coal left irrecoverably underground for every ton brought to the surface, but less than one-half of the economic value of coal is utilized by our primitive methods of consumption. In a time when it is possible to transform coal into gas and electricity at the mine and transport its fuel and power cheaply by pipe and wire, thirty per cent of our entire coal production is used for transportation by steam engines that harness up only from nine to twelve per cent of the energy in a ton of coal in a way that will actually pull a train—and a third of all the freight tonnage carried by the railroads is coal. Moreover our modern chemical industries, such as the dye industry, are based upon the substances contained in bituminous coal, most of which are wasted in our customary methods of consumption. These facts impose an immense burden of needless cost upon the consumer, and draw into the overexpanded coal industry tens of thousands of miners in excess of efficient requirements. The owners are therefore subject to wide fluctuations in the price of their product, the miners are the victims of intermittent and irregular employment with consequent uncertainty of earnings, and the public ultimately foots the bill, which, as has already been pointed out, Mr. F. G. Tryon of the U. S. Geological Survey calculates at one million dollars for each working day paid in unofficial and needless taxation, and the miners, by the terms of the collective agreement are explicitly debarred from all participation in the solution of these problems of management.

As a remedy, bituminous operators have proposed that they shall be relieved of the restrictions of the Sherman law, so that they may combine to limit production and regulate distribution and prices as the anthracite owners have succeeded in doing. The miners, by resolution of their national convention, have proposed a policy of public ownership and democratic administration, the entrusting of the technical regulation and development of the mines to engineers appointed by the government and the administration of labor relations by a democratic tribunal composed of representatives of the technical management, the public, and the miners. The effectiveness of either policy would be contingent upon the application to the mines and their product of the scientific knowledge which has been rapidly accumulating during the last decade and very little of which is now applied to the industry. The character of the political reconstruction of the industry, which public necessity must sooner or later compel, will be largely determined by the outcome of the impending technical revolution in the production and utilization of coal.

CHAPTER VIII
RIVALS OF COAL

Until recently it has been taken for granted that there was plenty of coal. The industrial revolution rose and triumphed on the theory of an inexhaustible supply. Mines were opened casually here and there and such coal as was easy to get was taken from the reserves which were supposed to be bottomless. And men were poured into the mines, thousands in excess of the need. They were as plentiful as the coal. Because of these two things—the vast amount of coal and the cheap and abundant man power—the coal industry came through the industrial revolution which it created, without being itself revolutionized.

Now the coal supply is large, but it is not by any means unlimited. No one can increase it. There is no way of manufacturing coal. The limitations of the supply were fixed by the geographical revolution. Twenty million years ago all the coal we have or shall have was packed away in the ribs of the earth in seams varying from sixty feet to the thickness of a blade of grass. It is estimated that we still have in the world more than seven thousand billion tons distributed as follows:

North America	5,073,431,000,000
Asia	1,279,586,000,000
Europe	784,190,000,000
Australasia	170,410,000,000
Africa	57,839,000,000
South America	32,097,000,000
Total	7,397,553,000,000

This seems like a vast amount which even wasteful production could hardly exhaust in thousands of years. But much of the supply is of such low grade as to be inefficient as a steam producer, much of it occurs at such deep levels or so remote from the centers of population as to be commercially unprofitable to mine. Mr. Floyd W. Parsons, formerly editor of the *Coal Age*, has warned us that "each year now witnesses the exhaustion of a number of high-grade coal areas. Far more mines producing better grades of coal are being worked out than there are new mines commencing to produce.... Operating companies are now going over their acreage, taking out pillars and working low-grade thin seams." And Mr. D. B. Rushmore, chief engineer in the power and mining department of the General Electric Company, calculates that if our coal consumption were to continue to increase at the apparently normal rate of seven per cent each year, the life of our known reserves would be as follows:

> Eastern District, which includes the most accessible
>   and best quality of our fuel   59 years
>
> Eastern, Central, and Southern Districts   65 years
>
> Entire U. S. and Alaska, two-thirds of this being low-
>   grade coals and lignites   84 years

These figures are based upon the appraisals of the U. S. Geological Survey. They include coal in veins as shallow as fourteen inches, all coal whose ash content does not exceed thirty per cent, and all known deposits within six thousand feet of the surface. They are based on the optimistic assumption that two-thirds of the coal in the mines will be brought to the surface, a considerably higher recovery than has hitherto been achieved. Mr. Rushmore concludes that the evidence points unmistakably to an approaching scarcity of high-grade coal and increasingly higher prices.

One of the greatest single causes of waste and increased prices is our antiquated system of distributing the energy contained in coal. It is estimated that every hundred tons of coal shipped involves the burning of ten tons in railroad locomotives. There is no longer any technical justification for transporting power in the enormously bulky form of coal when it could be much more efficiently distributed by pipe and wire in the form of gas and electricity. Even were it not enormously inefficient, there are definite physical limits beyond which the steam haulage of coal in bulk cannot be increased — certain bottle necks like that through which the Lehigh River flows, narrow edges like that along the Susquehanna, where no more slow puffing trains can go toiling up and down the slippery grades, because there is no more room for them on the tracks. Already the load upon the antiquated steam railroads is too heavy for them to bear, so that the system of transportation breaks down under every peak load and in every crisis such as that induced by the war.

Moreover our methods of consumption are incredibly wasteful. Mr. George Otis Smith, Director of the U. S. Geological Survey, has prepared a chart showing that of every two thousand pounds of coal, six hundred pounds are lost in mining, one hundred and twenty-six pounds are consumed at the mine and en route to the boiler room, four hundred and forty-six pounds are lost in gases going up the stack, fifty-one pounds are lost by radiation and fifty-one in the ash pit, six hundred and fifty pounds are lost in converting heat energy into mechanical energy, and only seventy-six pounds out of the two thousand are actually converted into productive mechanical energy. After two hundred years of mechanical invention, we are still stupidly content to dissipate ninety-six per cent of the labor-saving value of coal.

But even if the coal supply were unlimited, if every year a new crop grew to take the place of the one consumed, even if it were physically possible for the railroads to carry an ever-increasing load, the miners are not willing to get it out on the same old basis of low wages, high hazards, and demoralizing irregularity of employment. Man power has changed its own status. In 1919 the wages of common labor at the mines were fixed at seven and a half dollars a day. As wages go, this would have meant a reasonably fair standard of living if work in the mines had been steady. But during the last thirty years the mines have been idle an average of ninety-three days in every three hundred and eight working days in the year, and during 1921 the miner was fortunate who got as much as two days of work in the week, that is, fifteen dollars a week and seven hundred and eighty dollars a year. The hazards of mining have increased. The U. S. Bureau of Mines tells us that while in 1890 the death rate of coal miners was 2.15 for every thousand men employed, in 1914 the rate had increased to 3.19. In 1890 between three and four miners were killed for every million tons mined; in 1914 between four and five miners were killed for every million tons. Labor is no longer content to be sacrificed in order to put an increasing stream of cheap coal into the fire boxes of engines that waste nine-tenths and more of their labor and so deprive them of the possibility of the good life according to American standards. They are taking stock and evaluating themselves. Some of their demands, like the six-hour day, five days a week, are socially unwise, but they represent a just protest against the demoralizing intermittency of employment. The demand is simply an effort to spread the actual hours of work evenly throughout the year. Already the conditions imposed by the unions in the interest of a reasonable standard of living act as a strong differential against the mining of difficult seams and poor grades of coal. They are rapidly getting into a position where they can dictate the conditions under which they will hazard their lives underground. And these are not conditions which the coal industry with its competitive overdevelopment, its load of parasite railroads, sales companies, company-owned houses and stores, its inefficient operating methods, and particularly its antiquated energy-producing equipment on which it must pay heavy interest, is prepared to meet.

Because the supply of coal cannot much longer meet the cumulatively wasteful demands upon it; because the railroad system is breaking down under the increased bulk of coal to be transported; because the miners are increasingly insisting that the reward of their hazardous labor must give them a fair chance of the good life according to American standards of living; and because the community which must be served cannot indefinitely pay the price of inefficiency and waste, the present order in the coal industry is drawing to a close.

The technicians have seen this impending change for a long time. Through their help the industrial revolution might have reorganized the coal industry decades ago under the pressure of an increasing demand for power, if it had not been held off by new discoveries of petroleum and natural gas. Petroleum, which had been used in a small way in many countries for centuries, first became an international commodity when Roumania began to ship it in 1857. It took on great industrial importance when the first American well, the famous Drake well in Oil Creek, Pennsylvania, was sunk in 1859. But in 1860 the world's total recorded production was less than five hundred and ten thousand barrels, of which five hundred thousand barrels are credited to the United States. By 1917 the world output had risen to nearly four hundred and fifty million barrels, of which the United States furnished nearly four hundred million.

The coal and petroleum industries are closely interrelated. Coal and petroleum are largely interchangeable as sources of energy. Both can be used for fuel under boilers in their crude state, although crude oil is the more efficient; both provide an illuminating oil for use in lamps, although kerosene is so much better than coal oil as to have driven it out of the market; both furnish a satisfactory fuel for the internal-combustion engine, although benzol, a coal derivative, has not yet been recovered in sufficient quantities to make it a competitor of gasoline; both provide a fuel gas, although that derived from petroleum has the greater heat value. Ton for ton, petroleum has every advantage over coal, and there is every reason why it should drive coal out of its preeminent position in industry, except one—the limitations of the supply.

For petroleum is far cheaper to produce, not only in terms of money, but in terms of human effort and life. Compare with the labor and hazard of opening and working a coal mine Pogue and Gilbert's description of the opening of an oil well.

"Drilling an oil well is commonly done by means of a heavy string of tools, suspended at the end of a cable and given a churning motion by a walking beam rocked by a steam engine.... The steel tools, falling under their own weight, literally punch their way to the depth desired."

The usual custom is for four men working two twelve-hour shifts to sink a well. Their work is to keep the engine that operates the drill running, to watch the operation, and to stoke the engine. The only danger is when the time has come to "shoot" the well. This is done only if the oil does not flow naturally when the oil-bearing strata are reached. The "shooting" consists in dropping a "go devil" upon canisters of nitroglycerine to blow out a cavity at the bottom in which oil may collect. If the charge explodes before it reaches the bottom of the well, it may blow back and wreck the derrick, and the timbers and "bull-wheel" may fall upon the men. This danger, which can be obviated by the simple process of the men going away until after the charge has exploded, is practically the only one connected with drilling for petroleum, except for the incidental danger which all handling of high explosives necessarily involves.

A well costs only about one-tenth as much per foot of descent as a mine shaft; and it can be put down in much quicker time. When it is once in contact with the oil, operating expenses are trifling, for in many cases the oil reaches the surface under natural gas pressure, and in others it has merely to be pumped. There are not the expenses for breaking rock, timbering, or haulage, which are common in coal mining.

So that in addition to being a better fuel than coal to burn under a steam boiler, petroleum mining is as healthful and safe an occupation as can be well found in contrast with the extremely dangerous work of the coal miner, and it can be far more quickly and more cheaply got out of the ground.

It has other advantages.

Coal, bituminous coal especially, is so bulky and so liable to spontaneous combustion that it is difficult to store. Petroleum, on the contrary, can be easily and satisfactorily stored in iron tanks which, standing about like great cheese boxes, are characteristic of the oil-producing country. Added to the advantage of easy storage is the much greater one of easy transportation. Unlike coal, the crude petroleum supply of the country makes no demand upon the railroads. Only under exceptional circumstances and for short distances is it hauled about in tank cars. It has its own independent system of pipe lines, after the manner of a great water supply. These systems connect the oil wells with the refineries, the markets, and the seaports.

The pipe lines are ample to distribute the current production of oil. It is these pipe lines that have not only made the petroleum industry absolutely independent of the railroads, but through the low cost of their operation have lowered the cost of petroleum products. They have also made it possible to establish oil refineries near the points of consumption and have united widely separated fields.

For all these reasons—because it is a more efficient fuel under steam boilers; because it can be produced more cheaply; because the work of mining it is easy and the danger is slight; and because having an independent transportation system of its own it makes no demand on the already overburdened railroads—petroleum might have superseded coal as the power that rules industry if there had been enough of it. Even as it is, petroleum has been able to meet a large part of the demand for fuel and so stand between the coal industry and the reorganization hanging over it.

But we have been, if possible, more prodigal in our exploitation of our petroleum resources than of coal. There was an immediate market for all the petroleum that could be produced. The well-owner's chief anxiety was lest his neighbor, whose well tapped the same underground reservoir, should get the oil out before he did. So the exploiters of petroleum rushed on their quarry with an avidity never equalled by the exploiters of coal. While approximately one-half of the coal has been left in the ground through the eagerness of the owners to beat each other to market, from seventy to ninety per cent of the petroleum in the various fields has been lost from the same cause. And industry has seemed to take it for granted that because petroleum was being produced so rapidly, there was an unlimited supply. In 1916, many plants shifted from coal to fuel oil, because of the inability of the railroads to deliver coal. We have developed an oil-burning navy and are rapidly developing an oil-burning merchant marine. Ships and factory furnaces are competing with the internal-combustion engines of millions of automobiles and the hungry lamps of the countryside for the diminishing reserves of petroleum. Already the supply of crude petroleum is hard pressed by the demand for fuel oil. Already approximately one-half of the original petroleum supply of the United States is gone. In 1918, 460,721,000 barrels were taken, while it was estimated that 6,730,000,000 barrels remained in the ground, and the production during the two subsequent years was approximately 400,000,000 barrels annually. The petroleum reserve, converting barrels into tons, amounts to only $\frac{2}{1000}$ of our reserves of coal. If we stopped mining coal tomorrow and let American petroleum take its place, all our petroleum resources would be exhausted in about fifteen months.

And even if the supply of petroleum were far less limited than the experts estimate it to be, even if there were enough of it to last for many decades to come, the fact that it is practically the one lubricant of the industrial world makes it a social crime to burn it as a substitute for coal. Without it, every railroad wheel would run hot and stop; the great turbines in our ships and modern power plants move on bearings that are smothered in petroleum oil. And for petroleum as a lubricant there is no commercially available substitute.

Closely associated with petroleum and originally derived from it, is natural gas. There is no way of telling how great the supply of this has been in the past, how much there is in reserve, or what the present outflow is, because the waste of natural gas has been and is notorious. We do know, however, that the per capita consumption in 1915, according to the U. S. Geological Survey, was approximately four times the consumption of artificial gas, and seven times that of the by-product coke-oven gas, and that its average price to the consumer was sixteen cents a thousand cubic feet as against ninety-one cents for artificial gas and ten cents for coke-oven gas. About one-third of the natural gas is used for domestic purposes, about two-thirds is used for manufacture. It is conservatively estimated that 100,000,000 gallons of gasoline can be recovered from it annually and it is the primary source of the lamp black from which all the printers' ink in present use is made. The supply of natural gas in reserve is not calculable, but since most of the wells show a diminished flow, it is believed to be on the way to exhaustion.

Although the supplies of oil and gas have supplemented coal for half a century and protected the coal industry from the same sort of economic pressure which has forced reorganization upon most other enterprises, the time is at hand when they can no longer do so.

The imaginative appeal of hydroelectric power has led many people to hope that water-power electricity would come to the aid of coal and possibly replace it. But Mr. Charles P. Steinmetz, of the General Electric Company, tells us that the total available water power of the United States has been variously estimated at from fifty to one hundred million horse-power, that is, from one-sixth to one-third of the horse-power equivalent of our present annual coal production. He has gone further and calculated the maximum possible value of all water power beyond which the ultimate skill of invention could never possibly go. If every raindrop which falls anywhere in the United States, allowing only for the amount of water needed by agriculture and the loss due to seepage and evaporation, were collected and all the power which it could develop in its journey to the sea were efficiently utilized, the resultant energy would amount to just about the same as the total which we get out of our present coal consumption for all purposes. Water power— hydroelectric energy—can never replace coal.

The waste of both petroleum and gas has been largely due to the unrestrained acquisitive instinct seeking quick wealth in response to the cry of the steam engine for more and more fuel. They were drafted into service because they could do the work of coal and do it more efficiently. But their diminishing supply makes it impossible for them longer to stave off the impending technical revolution in the coal industry. The miners are growing restive under the evils of intermittent employment, uncertain income, and demoralizing conditions of living. The public begins to rebel against irregularity of supply and ruinously high prices. The antiquated transportation system creaks and staggers under a load which the advance of technical science makes it unnecessary for it longer to carry.

All these, taken together with the still-increasing demand for power to drive on production and pile up a surplus on which to base an advancing civilization, are forcing a new technical revolution upon the coal industry.

CHAPTER IX
THE TECHNICAL REVOLUTION

The economic surplus which the industrial revolution of the latter eighteenth century created was the product of a crude, extensive exploitation of our natural resources. With the aid of the steam engine men skimmed the cream of the mines, the forests, and the new soil of the American continent.

The wasteful use of our coal, paralleling as it did our increasing need for power, was hampering the industries of the country even before the war. After the breaking out of the conflict the overwhelming pressure for increased production could not be met. In a panic we pushed our old methods of coal exploitation further than ever before, drew on our oil and gas supplies to the utmost, and then in final desperation integrated the administrative side of the coal industry through the Fuel Administration.

The relief this brought was immediate, although the chief work of the Fuel Administration was merely to systematize and coordinate the distribution of coal so that those who must have it would get it. For during wartime the factories must run, and the autocratic integration which the Fuel Administration accomplished created a seeming abundance by keeping the factory wheels of at least the essential industries turning.

But the relief was only apparent—not actual. When the tumult of the war was over and we were back in still water, Secretary Lane announced that the enormous development of war industries had created an almost insatiable demand for power—a demand that was overreaching the available supply with such rapidity that had hostilities continued, it is certain that by 1920 we should have been facing an extreme power shortage. Integrated administration had done all it could but the problem of power to advance civilization—to build up a surplus through production—to give all men the chance of the good life, was still unsolved. Just as the integration by the Fuel Administration had deferred the acute power shortage during the war, so the business depression that followed the signing of the armistice is still holding it in check. And yet if civilization is to go on, our multitudinous factory wheels must turn again more swiftly and in increasing number, our looms must weave more and more cloth, and new cars and new ships must carry new millions of people to and fro. As yet we know no other material means through which to build up the good life than these whirling wheels.

The technical experts have agreed that the problem must be solved through the integration of all our sources of fuel and power which they, like the Fuel Administration during the war, regard as a common reservoir like the water supply of a modern community, and through the reduction of both coal and water power to terms of their common denominator, electricity. As the result of Secretary Lane's prevision of the impending power shortage, Congress in 1921 made an appropriation for a preliminary survey by the technical experts of the power resources along the Atlantic seaboard from Washington to Boston and for one hundred and fifty miles inland. This territory has been called the "finishing shop" of America. It is of irregular coast line, giving good harbors for the shipping to carry its products overseas; its swift streams turned the first factory wheels in America; its mountain ranges are full of metals and easily accessible coal; and to this region the industrially trained peoples of Europe most naturally come. Obviously its factory wheels must turn.

As a result of the survey of this region, engineers have worked out what is called the Superpower Plan. According to this, a giant network of wire will be woven over the territory between the Alleghenies and the Atlantic seaboard and charged with the very essence of power. Great steel towers, like those that now carry the currents generated at Niagara Falls, the Keokuk Dam on the Mississippi, and the Roosevelt Dam at the head of Salt River in the Arizona Desert, will stride through the valleys and across the mountains along a two-hundred-foot right of way. Instead of steel rails and puffing engines to convey industrial power, there will be only towers and copper wires. Instead of millions of tons of raw coal moving slowly along through bottle necks in the mountains and through congested freight yards, there will be the silent rush of uncounted electrons hurrying to the centers of production to do the work of man. Instead of spreading dirt and noise and ugliness, these new carriers of cosmic energy will be high harps for the wind.

According to this plan of the Superpower Commission the main line of this new power system begins at Washington and follows the coast through the great centers of population—Baltimore, Wilmington, Philadelphia, Newark, New York, New Haven, Providence, Boston, and on up to Newburyport. Stretching away from this main line two principal inland lines are projected, one swinging off at Baltimore out to Harrisburg and up the anthracite valley to Scranton; another leaving the main line just before it reaches New York and stretching up the Hudson Valley to Poughkeepsie, Port Jervis, and Utica, tapping the hydroelectric generating stations in the Adirondacks, and connecting again through Pittsfield, Northampton, and Worcester with the main line in Boston. North and south cross lines mesh these secondary lines with the main line along the coast—one through Hartford and Waterbury to New Haven, and another from Worcester to Providence, with a short branch line to New Bedford. Back and forth across this network of high-tension wires will run the power to turn the factory wheels.

About nine-tenths of this power will be the developed energy of coal. The Superpower Commission's plan calls for the establishment of great steam-generating plants near the mines where the coal will be used to fire steam engines which will turn dynamos and so convert the energy of coal into electricity and feed it to that great harp in the wind. Steam-generating plants to supply more distant consumers are projected at tidewater—that is at places to which coal can be delivered by coastwise steamers. Incidentally these tidewater plants involve a considerable amount of coal haulage from the mines to the seaports, and from the ports nearest the mines to the other ports along the coast; from the lower West Virginia fields, across the mountains, to the southern end of Chesapeake Bay and thence by boat northward along the coast to Connecticut, Rhode Island, Massachusetts, and New Hampshire. En route this coal will be joined by other coal from the upper West Virginia and the lower Pennsylvania bituminous fields and also by coal from the middle Pennsylvania field which will have to be freighted through New Jersey to the Hudson ports, then again up Long Island Sound by steamdrawn barges. While great economies would be effected by the transformation of coal into electric energy at the superpower stations, both at the mines and at the tidewater ports, the plan of the Superpower Commission still involves the necessity of hauling millions of tons of raw coal from the mines to seaboard. This limitation the Commission held to be necessary, not only for the purpose of utilizing the comparatively small plants which existing public utility companies have already built, but because at the time their report was made the electrical engineers had not yet perfected means of transporting electricity for long distances without great leakage on the way. Since the Commission's survey was published, however, an invention has been announced which greatly increases the distance over which the high-voltage currents can be efficiently sent, so that it is now feasible to transmute a much larger proportion of coal into electricity at the mine. The plan for practically all the tidewater generating plants can be given up, together with the long, slow, costly process of carrying coal to them, and that ninety per cent of the electricity for the superpower system which is derived from coal can be generated directly at the mine.

The other ten per cent according to the Commission's plan will be hydroelectric power. Generating stations are to be established at the rapids of the Potomac just above Washington; along the lower reaches of the Susquehanna in Pennsylvania and Maryland; along the upper courses of the Delaware and the Hudson; in the Adirondacks; and at intervals along the whole length of the Connecticut River. But the main dependence of the projected superpower system is still the bituminous coal supply which it is planned to keep at its old job of raising steam to drive the turbine engines which will in turn drive the electric dynamos.

Besides the Commission's superpower plan for the Atlantic seaboard, other power systems have been sketched out, one centering around Helena in southern Illinois and designed to serve most of the Mississippi Valley, one near the northwest coast, another in California.

The integration of water and coal is a long step toward the solution of the power problem, in that it not only brings a new force to supplement the coal supply but also saves the coal now used by steam locomotives to haul raw fuel to its millions of consumers. Moreover, it contemplates the electrification of all the railroads within the zone whose traffic is heavy enough to warrant it, and as it is estimated that two pounds of coal applied to an electric locomotive will do as much work as seven and one-half to eight and one-half pounds when applied to a steam locomotive, the amount of coal now used for transportation will be still further reduced. Through such beginnings as these projected superpower systems must come the comprehensive integration of the industry.

But the Federal Commission's superpower plan as published is only a beginning. It is not enough merely to save the energy of coal, to relieve the congestion on the freight railroads, and to provide a common-carrier system for high-voltage electricity. There is needed also the more intensive utilization of the fuel supply. The plan of the Superpower Commission regards coal—bituminous coal especially—as nothing more than fuel. The industrial revolution was built upon the power of coal to fire the boilers in steam engines. But the use of coal for the generation of steam only is almost the least efficient way in which it can be utilized. From the point of view of national economy the better utilization of what are known as the by-product values of bituminous coal is quite as important as the establishment of an integrated power system.

For coal is much more than potential power. Bituminous coal is the source of many of our most valuable mineral products and yet today, of the more than 500,000,000 tons annually produced, almost all is used exclusively for the production of power and all of its ingredients except the heat-producing elements are wasted. About one-twelfth of the bituminous coal—that which is now used for the production of coke in ovens that recover its by-product—must be excepted from this statement. Moreover, the 90,000,000 tons of anthracite mined every year are economically used because anthracite contains practically nothing but carbon and ash and its direct burning is the most efficient way in which it can be used if its energy content is thoroughly conserved. Omitting, then, the whole of the anthracite supply, and that bituminous which is already properly utilized, we still have more than 400,000,000 tons wastefully used every year—so wastefully that not only are all its commodity values destroyed, but its primary purpose of creating heat and industrial power is imperfectly served. In the effective integration of fuel and power it will become necessary to separate the energy-producing elements in bituminous coal—and also of the sub-bituminous coal, of lignite and peat, of which we have reserves amounting to the billions of tons—from those which have only a commodity value.

In their report made for the Smithsonian Institution, Gilbert and Pogue point out that "there are in one ton of good bituminous coal, fifteen hundred pounds of smokeless fuel analogous to anthracite, ten thousand cubic feet of gas, twenty-two pounds of ammonium sulphate, two and one-half gallons of benzol, and nine gallons of tar" and that lignite gives almost as much of these commodities. Apart from the fuel values represented by the "smokeless fuel analogous to anthracite" the gas and benzol, the ammonium sulphate, and tar have unique values as fertilizers, and the source of those mineral elements from which our dyes and a large part of our modern medicines are made. The process used to extract these commodity values is similar to that which nature used in making anthracite, except that the volatile matter which the geological revolution drove off into the air is collected and utilized.

The gas created by the process can be delivered by pipe lines over practically any distance to the centers of consumption, or, with the help of the internal-combustion engine, converted into electrical energy at the mine. Gas as a fuel has the great advantage that it eliminates both storage and haulage, and produces the same amount of heat from about one-half the amount of coal, and since it can be produced as needed all the year round it will go far to eliminate the seasonal character of coal mining. Moreover, wherever heat rather than light or power is desired, gas, in the present state of technical development, is even more economical than electricity. Under the by-product system the present annual coal output can be made to more than double its service in driving machinery and in addition it can be made to contribute heavily to our supply of fertilizers, motor fuel, and chemical products. It is estimated that the aggregate loss resulting from the present wasteful utilization of coal is over ten dollars a year for each inhabitant of the United States.

The by-products of coal can play an important part in the fuel industry. Where it is thoroughly integrated they can help in financing the development of hydro-electricity to supplement the electricity produced from coal. For while the running expenses of a hydroelectric plant are little more than the interest on the capital invested, the amount of that capital is large. Also the establishment of gas plants at the mines is a costly thing. The temptation is to revamp and repair and reorganize the present outworn and wasteful system rather than make large new investments and scrap the old equipment. But in the commercial value of the by-products from bituminous coal lies the possibility of paying for the new power to turn our factory wheels by the sale of dyes and fertilizer and medicines and tar and explosives and perfumes and a hundred other things. So it is to the chemical laboratories that we look for the new values which may make a superpower system financially possible just as it is to the electrical workshop that we look for the inventions which will integrate it into one thing.

But even the recovery and sale of the by-products of coal are not all that is involved in the new way of supplying the world with power. While gas can yield the full fuel value of coal in a more efficient form than solid fuel, as well as all the commodity values, if it is converted into power through the steam engine, at least one-half of its energy value is lost. To conserve its full value, gas must be burned in the internal-combustion engine, the most familiar type of which is the one we know under the hood of the automobile and the most efficient type is the Diesel engine which has made the by-product system industrially practical.

The internal-combustion engine is a relatively simple device for transforming the energy in fuel into power directly instead of indirectly as the steam engine does, of turning wheels at first hand, of cutting out steam as a middleman. It greatly enlarges the range of fuel utilization because it can burn not only fuel gas and the lighter oils—gasoline, benzol, and their close kin—but also fuel alcohol, the supply of which though hitherto only slightly developed will last as long as the sun and rain make vegetation grow in the soil. Our future success in winning and holding an economic surplus upon which the opportunity for the good life and a world civilization depends, rests almost as largely upon the internal-combustion engine as the industrial revolution depended upon the steam engine of Newcomen and Watt.

When the internal-combustion engine has been adequately developed, and that time is near at hand, it will be economically possible to establish the great superpower stations at the mines, to integrate the electricity flowing from their gas-driven dynamos with the flow from the hydroelectric stations on the great rivers and mountain streams, and to use the surplus gas and smokeless coal to supply the domestic consumer during the period of transition from our present wasteful fuel and power system to the new system which will give us heat and power with the turn of a button on an electric switch.

In our solution of the fuel problem there must be an extension of such work as that of the Fuel Administration which integrated the administrative side of the industry as by a man in a high tower with all the resources and needs of the country spread beneath him. He must see all the sources of power as in a common reservoir—all the coal and oil and gas and water power—all the fuel alcohol and those subtle forces within the material atoms themselves which scientists dream of forcing to do the work of man. He must sort and deliver power to fill the need, this in the form of oil or gas sent through its own pipe line; this still in the bulky form of coal or coke by rail or water to those few industries which can take no substitute; and more and more of it transmuted into electricity and poured along the singing wires, or later perhaps through the pathways of the air itself, to turn the wheels of industry.

And in addition to the actual pooling of the power resources of the country, there must come their intensive and economical use—economical by more standards than that of money alone—so that the miner who blasts the coal from the face, the man who sinks the oil well or runs the internal-combustion engine or strings the electric wires, will get in return for the thousands of tons of coal he has mined or the kilowatt hours he has generated from his dynamo, the material basis of the good life.

This integrated industry of which the mining of coal, the projected superpower systems, the pumping of oil, the development of water power, and the organization and training of those who produce or consume power are essential parts, is the inevitable result of the development that has gone before. Just as the industrial revolution had its beginnings in the coordination of the steam engine, the coal mines, and the factory machinery, and its incentive in the drive of the acquisitive instinct to make existence possible; so this new industrial advance, the integration of the power that drives industry, is the logical result of the development of long-distance electric transmission, the intense utilization of the fuel supply, and the invention of the internal-combustion engine, and it may result not only in making existence possible but in making life good.

CHAPTER X

THE STRAIT GATE

Since the days when the cosmic energy of coal was first harnessed to the looms of England, mechanical contrivances of almost miraculous ingenuity have followed one another in such rapid succession that men have come to place undue reliance upon machinery for the solution of the difficult human problems that impede progress toward the good life and a worthy civilization. Just as the earlier generations failed in the spiritual preparedness necessary to the conversion of the technical triumphs of Newcomen and Watt, Fulton and Stephenson, and a host of others to the higher ends of civilization, so our generation shows a similar disposition to rely upon the wonder workers of mechanical science to save us from the disastrous consequences of muddling along in the field of human relations whether in industry, in the nation, or among the nations. But the good life is not to be won by mechanical invention alone. One of the outstanding lessons of the World War was that great inventions in the realm of the physical and chemical sciences may be destructive of the very civilization which it is their higher mission to serve. Unless we have the spiritual capacity to make the technique of science obedient to the commandment to love our neighbor as ourselves, superpower systems, high-voltage transmission, the internal-combustion engine, may again intensify the exploitation of man by man, the clash of groups for power, the brutality of international wars for possession.

We men and women of the twentieth century have developed a complacent habit of priding ourselves upon our scientific open-mindedness, our respect for facts, our eagerness to accept the revelations of authentic scientific investigation and experiment. As we mount into the clouds on the wings of the aeroplane or catch the voice of the radio operator out of ethereal space, we have a tremendous sense of intellectual emancipation, a thrill of escape from ancient bigotries and superstitions. There is some warrant for this self-congratulatory attitude in so far as it relates to the physical sciences. We have reason to be proud that we have banished the primitive fears that led an earlier age to persecute men like Galileo for telling the truth with respect to the place of the earth in the stellar universe. We are sufficiently emancipated to know that the inventors of the dynamo, the turbine engine, the spectroscope, wireless telegraphy, and high-voltage electrical transmission are not guilty of heresy. When Steinmetz forges a thunderbolt and sends it crashing across his laboratory, we do not burn him for witchcraft. The inquirers into the nature of the atom, the structure of the cerebral ganglia, or the chemical composition of the nebulae in the Milky Way are free from medieval taboos.

But unfortunately we have not developed an equally enlightened attitude toward the inquirers into the nature of human relations in politics or industry, or toward those who would apply the experimental method to the development and scientific reconstruction of industrial or political government. Terms like *trusts, the money power, trade unions, industrial autocracy, collective bargaining, socialism, bolshevism, private monopoly, public ownership*, stir all our ancient fears, resentments, and hates. Men may be unorthodox in the physical sciences; we are growing tolerant of unorthodoxy in religious opinion. But unorthodoxy in the realm of politics is still frowned upon. We still imprison men for their political and economic opinions when they challenge the finality of accepted institutions and especially when they advocate the fundamental reconstruction of accepted forms of political and economic government. Yet it is quite as true in the realm of human relations, as in that of the physical sciences, that the truth and the truth only can make us free. Human brotherhood can be achieved only through human understanding.

It is a commonplace to say that the vigorous growth of democracy depends upon education. But much repetition has dulled the vital implications of the assertion. We tend to forget that a democracy that permits essential knowledge to be withheld from general circulation digs its own grave; that while men talk of emancipation and freedom, ignorance may forge chains for their enslavement. When any group within the community is permitted to treat facts essential to the development of right human relations as "trade secrets," education itself becomes stereotyped and sterile. Text-books and "lessons" become spiritually and intellectually empty, like the prayers which certain Eastern cults pin to wheels that spin idly in the wind.

The authentic prophets of democracy have constantly striven to keep the channels of popular education free from the clogging muck of selfishness, superstition, and prejudice. They have had faith in the essential justice and ultimate wisdom of informed public opinion. Such men have appeared in government, among the coal owners, among the miners, who are the commoners of the coal industry.

In 1914 the coal operators of Illinois and Indiana issued a *Statement of Facts* for the enlightenment of the Government and the people. The normal state of the coal industry, they declared, was such as to "endanger the lives of the miners, waste the coal reserves, and deprive the operators of any hope of profit." They therefore appealed for "appropriate and definite governmental control" to the extent "at least of permitting all their activities to be known to the public." They thus approved of the action of Congress in creating the Federal Trade Commission "to gather and compile information concerning, and to investigate from time to time the organization, business, conduct, practices, and management of any corporation engaged in commerce ... and to make public from time to time such portions of the information obtained by it, except trade secrets and names of customers, as it shall deem expedient in the public interest." The coal operators went further than Congress since they made no reservations with respect to trade secrets. But after the armistice, the organized operators of the nation, through one of their members, secured an injunction restraining the Federal Trade Commission from prosecuting its work of investigation and publicity, the effect of which was to render the Federal Trade Commission Act null and void so far as the education of the public with respect to the coal industry was concerned. In the language of a senator, this action "tied the Government's hands and poked out its eyes."

With a view to remedying certain of the major evils that interfered with the service of the coal industry to the nation, Senators Calder, Frelinghuysen, and Kenyon introduced bills and conducted public hearings. They had concluded that what Congress and the public needed to know if they were to legislate fairly and intelligently was the full truth about "ownership, production, distribution, stocks, investments, costs, sales, margins, and profits in the coal industry and trade." But in 1921, the organized operators of the country, feeling that they could conduct the industry most successfully without governmental supervision or the scrutiny of informed public opinion, opposed all attempts at legislation designed to accomplish the precise ends which in 1914 the operators of Illinois and Indiana regarded as essential to the best interests of all concerned. In reviewing the history of the efforts which he and his colleagues had made to get at and publish the facts, Senator Frelinghuysen reported to Congress that "though we made every concession that we felt justified in making, we find, after two years of conference and the price of coal still high, that practically all of these operators, organized and unorganized, are bitterly opposing the principle of these two bills—first, the season freight rate bill, and second the bill 'to aid in stabilizing the coal industry'— and have organized an elaborate propaganda with a view to bringing about their defeat.... The National Coal Association has been the chief defender of the coal trade since I became interested in the subject.... For a time I looked upon the men of this organization as fair and reasonable and I sympathized with their demand that the coal trade be permitted to work out its own salvation without Government interference, provided full statistics were obtainable regarding cost of production, transportation, and delivery to the humblest consumer. For a time they seemed willing to concede this. But I am finally and reluctantly convinced that my hope in that direction has always been a delusion."

After devoting two years to a vain attempt to get at "full statistics," Senator Frelinghuysen lost patience with the operators. But he forgot that many of their leaders still sincerely adhere to Mr. Baer's faith that God has entrusted the interests of the community to the owners of property and that congressional interference, even when limited to the ascertainment of statistics, is subversive not only of the status of the owners as trustees of the nation's fuel resources, but also of the public interest itself. This conviction of the operators is a fact that must be weighed without impatience like any fact in chemistry or physics.

The position of many labor leaders is fundamentally the same as that of the operators. They have the traditional fear of the autocratic power which they believe to be inherent in the state. Like the operators, they are convinced that the public interest is best served when each and all of the groups within industry are left free to pursue their special interests with utmost aggressiveness, on the theory that the clash of many selfishnesses results, as by a law of nature, in the neutralization of selfishness and its conversion into public advantage. It is utopian folly, they say, to attempt to change "human nature," the dominant characteristic of which they hold to be the acquisitive instinct, and equally vain to attempt to modify the natural operation of the "law of supply and demand," which, in their judgment, transcends the "idealistic" law of service. They agree that it is unfortunate that this should be so, but since it is so, does it not behoove practical men to act accordingly? There are many men of this mind among the leaders and rank and file of the miners, as well as among the operators.

But the creative impulse back of the organized labor movement is by virtue of necessity the democratic impulse, and where the democratic impulse is vigorous it feeds upon the consciousness of kind whose principal channel of growth is knowledge. In their national convention, held in Cleveland, Ohio, in 1919, the miners adopted a resolution calling upon the Government, "through Act of Congress, to acquire title to the coal properties within the United States now owned by private interests; by purchasing said properties at a figure representing the actual valuation of said properties, as determined upon investigation by accredited agents of the federal Government." They asked that "the coal mining industry be operated by the federal Government and that the miners be given equal representation upon such councils or commissions as may be delegated the authority to administer the affairs of the coal mining industry...." The stated object of the resolution was to secure the operation of the industry "in the interest of, and for the use and comfort of all of the people of the commonwealth ..." and "to prevent the profligate waste that is taking place under private ownership of these resources by having the Government take such steps as may be necessary providing for the nationalization of the coal mining industry of the United States."

As to the relative merits of the policy of national ownership as advocated by the United Mine Workers of America, and the policy of free competition and unrestrained private initiative advocated by the organized operators, it is for the informed public ultimately to judge. For two years, the miners' nationalization resolution stood as the expression of a more or less vague aspiration, a more or less vague faith that public ownership would check overdevelopment and so eliminate the humanly demoralizing effects of intermittent production and irregularity of employment. Nationalization, the miners believed, would go far to correct the disastrous moral and physical effects of a situation which on an average of ninety-three days in each working year, deprives them of the opportunity to work.

At their next national convention, held in Indianapolis in 1921, they themselves recognized the controversial nature of their nationalization policy. So they moved to less debatable ground. They created a Nationalization Research Committee to get at and secure the publication of facts. In his first public address as chairman of this Nationalization Research Committee, Mr. John Brophy, president of the organized miners in district No. 2, Central Pennsylvania, instead of dogmatizing about the miners' policy of public ownership and democratic administration as the infallible remedy for the evils of the coal industry, appealed to the public, the operators, and the miners "to stop theoretical squabbling and cooperate with us in making all facts about the industry available to the public. We believe in intelligently planned industry. We believe that the only method for the intelligent organization of the industry is nationalization. The employers disagree. In order to arrive at a decision we ask them to submit the facts to the American people, the only jury that has a right to pass judgment on the case…. We ask immediate legislation for centralized, continuous, and compulsory fact-finding in the coal industry."

A democracy that acquiesces in its own ignorance of the elementary facts respecting an industry upon which, not only its own economic life, but also the economic life and civilized progress of the entire world so largely depends, betrays the high privilege and responsibility of a self-governing citizenship. Today neither the public nor the Government knows whether the coal industry is fairly capitalized, what the extent and value of the coal reserves are, whether depreciation and depletion charges are reasonable, or what are the profits and losses of the industry. Nobody knows whether the prices which the consumer is required to pay are fair and reasonable. Nobody knows precisely what the preventable wastes of the industry are. The annual wages of the miners are not subject to precise statistical statement, nor does anyone know the number of hours the miners work when the mines are in operation or the number of hours they are given opportunity to work. The statements we have are for the most part large averages based upon inductions from small cross-sections of the industry. The working conditions of the miners, the technical state of the organization of work underground, the cost of living at the more than eleven thousand mines, remain in the foggy realm of guesswork, estimate, and speculation. In the face of conditions which, as the operators of Illinois and Indiana stated in 1914, "endanger the lives of the miners, waste the coal reserves, and deprive the operators of any hope of profit," the people, like the people's government, are ignorantly helpless. In the absence of essential information, the public especially at times of controversy within the industry is left to the mercy of prejudiced and partisan propaganda.

"I think it is plain folly," Dr. Garfield, formerly head of the Fuel Administration, testified before the Senate Committee on Manufactures, "not to provide for a continuous finding of the facts as to the cost of production, as to the stocks of coal on hand, as to the working conditions in the mines, and as to the cost of living…. We cannot get along as a Government or as an industry, whether you think of it from the standpoint of the operators or mine workers, without knowing the facts, and the public is also vitally interested in these facts."

The U. S. Geological Survey has in the past issued:

1. Annual report on the production of coal by counties and by producing fields. 2. Annual report on the movement of coal, showing the state or locality to which coal produced in each district is shipped; and the origin, by producing fields, of the coal consumed in each state or locality. 3. Current reports at frequent intervals, showing production of coal, operating conditions at the mines, and the movement of coal by rail and by water to various consuming districts. 4. Occasional reports on stocks of coal in the hands of representative consumers. 5. Annual reports on consumption by the larger users. 6. Special reports.

But while the methods to be used in these reports have been worked out, not all of them are being carried on permanently, the reason being lack of funds. The latest detailed annual report on the movement of coal is for 1918, and it is uncertain when another can be prepared. The current reports are inadequate and the reports on stocks and consumption are issued only at irregular intervals.

Even the annual reports of production leave untouched many subjects of vital importance. We have no quantitative information, on a national scale, as to the amount of coal cleaned; the amount of mine-run, slack, and prepared sizes produced; the mechanical equipment of the mines; the depth of the coal workings; the distance the miner must traverse from mine mouth to working face; the dip of the coal seam; the tonnage produced by long-wall or room-and-pillar methods; the quantity of coal in the ground lost to the nation each year, in the roof, in pillars, because of squeezes; or the quantity lost in thin seams not now minable which are broken and fractured by the mining of lower seams. We do not know accurately how fast electrical haulage is replacing animal haulage underground, what progress the loading machine is making in relieving human backs of the labor of shoveling coal into cars. Of course, any operator and any miner knows of these things in a general way in his own locality, but such scattered, hazy, local knowledge will not suffice. We must have accurate information, national in scope.

In the realm of the financing of coal companies the ignorance of the public is almost complete. We do not know the capital value of the coal deposits, nor the degree of concentration and control of ownership of mines or mineral. We do not even know who owns the coal beds. There is no list of the landholding companies who as landlords absorb in many districts the economic rent paid by the mines working favorable seams. We do not know the prevailing royalty rates, we do not know whether or not there is a soft-coal trust. The most basic of our American industries moves in fog by day and blackness by night.

The social creeds of the Christian churches will remain the expressions of vague aspirations until they are supplemented by the knowledge essential to their concrete definition. Men and women who profess allegiance to the Great Commandments of Jesus have come to realize that the Kingdom of God on Earth, the Brotherhood of Man, cannot be built by fiat or verbal proclamation. The building of a worthy civilization is as definitely an engineering enterprise as the building of the Panama Canal. It demands a scientific procedure and a patient devotion as thoroughgoing as that which during the past two hundred years has gone into the development of the steam engine, the aeroplane, or high-tension electric transmission. The theory of nationalization, like the theory of collective bargaining and the traditional theory of progress by free competition, must each be tested, as the existing social and industrial order must be tested, in the light of painfully ascertained facts, and in terms of their effect upon the individual personality.

For it is only in the light of the truth that we shall be able to build a civilization in which the individual personality may find full fruition. It is only by the aid of knowledge and human understanding that we shall be able to resolve the drama of civilization into a victory of the consciousness of kind over the warfaring acquisitive instinct. It is only by making the technique of science obedient to the Great Commandments of Jesus that we shall be able to build a civilization worthy of a world that moves through infinite space with the sun and the marching stars.

BIBLIOGRAPHY

WHAT TO READ

A SELECT LIST

American Economic Review. New Haven, Conn.
Supplement. March, 1921.

ARCHBALD, HUGH
Four-Hour Day in Coal. N. Y. H. W. Wilson Co. 1922. 148 pp.

BLOCH, LOUIS
Coal Miners' Insecurity; Facts about Irregularity of Employment in the Bituminous Coal Industry in the United States. N. Y. Russell Sage Foundation. 1922. 50 pp.

BROPHY, JOHN
See United Mine Workers of America, District No. 2, and United Mine Workers of America, Nationalization Research Committee.

CAMPBELL, M. R.
Coal Fields of the United States. Wash. Govt. Printing Office. 1917. 33 pp. (U. S. Geological Survey. Prof. paper. 100–4.) Map, tables, diagrams.

COMMONS, J. R., ed.
Trade Unionism and Labor Problems, 2d series. Boston. Ginn & Co. 1921. 838 pp.
Contains:
Edgar Sydenstricker. Settlement of Disputes under Agreement in the Anthracite Industry. pp. 495–524.
Ethelbert Stewart. Equalizing Competitive Conditions. pp. 525–533.

COMMONS, J. R., and others
History of Labour in the United States. N. Y. Macmillan Co. 1918. 2 vols.

ECKEL, E. C.
Coal, Iron and War; A Study in Industrialism, Past and Future. N. Y. Henry Holt & Co. 1920. 375 pp.

EVANS, CHRIS.
History of the United Mine Workers of America from the Year 1860 to 1900.

Indianapolis. United Mine Workers of America. 1920. 2 vols.

GIBBINS, H. DE B.
Economic and Industrial Progress of the Century. Phila. Bradley-Garretson Co., Ltd. 1903. 524 pp.

GIDDINGS, F. H.
Principles of Sociology. N. Y. Macmillan Co.

GILBERT, C. G., and POGUE, J. E.
America's Power Resources; the Economic Significance of Coal, Oil and Water Power. N. Y. Century Co. 1921. 326 pp.

GREAT BRITAIN. Coal Industry Commission
Reports and Minutes of Evidence. London. H. M. Stationery Office. 1919. 3 vols. (Cmd. 359–361.)

HAMMOND, J. L., and BARBARA
Skilled Labourer, 1760–1832. N. Y. Longmans, Green & Co. 1919. 397 pp.
Town Labourer, 1760–1832. N. Y. Longmans, Green & Co. 1918. 346 pp.
Village Labourer, 1760–1832; A New Civilization. N. Y. Longmans, Green & Co. 1921. 342 pp.

HAPGOOD, POWERS
In Non-Union Mines; the Diary of a Coal Digger. N. Y. Bureau of Industrial Research. 1922. 48 pp.

HODGES, FRANK
Nationalization of the Mines. N. Y. Thomas Seltzer. Prof. d. 1920.

LANE, W. D.
Civil War in West Virginia; A Story of the Industrial Conflict in the Coal Mines. N. Y. B. W. Huebsch. 1921. 128 pp.

LAUCK, W. J.
Summary, Analysis and Statement Before the United States Anthracite Coal Commission. Wash. United Mine Workers of America. 1920. 44 pp.
The Trade Union as the Basis for Collective Bargaining, a Compilation of Sanctions and Experiences. Wash. United Mine Workers of America. 1920. 171 pp.
What a Living Wage Should Be as Determined by Authoritative Budget Studies. Wash. United Mine Workers of America. 1920. 7 pp.

MITCHELL, JOHN
Organized Labor, Its Problems, Purposes and Ideals and the Present and Future of American Wage Earners. Phila. American Book and Bible House. 1903. 436 pp.

Moore, E. S.
 Coal; its Properties, Analysis, Classification, Geology, Extraction, Uses and
  Distribution. N. Y. John Wiley & Sons. 1922. 462 pp.

Murray, W. S., and others
 Superpower System for the Region between Boston and Washington. Wash.
  Govt. Printing Office. 1921. 261 pp. (U. S. Geological Survey, Professional
  Paper. 123.)

Roy, Andrew
 **History of the Coal Miners of the United States, from the Development of
  the Mines to the Close of the Anthracite Strike of 1902.** Columbus, O. J.
  L. Trauger Printing Co. 1907.

Saward, Frederick W.
 Saward's Annual; a standard statistical review of the coal trade, by Frederick
  W. Saward. N. Y. 1922. 254 pp. 1907.

Shaler, N. S.
 Man and the Earth. N. Y. Chautauqua Press. 1907. 240 pp.

Spur, J. E., ed.
 Political and Commercial Geology and the World's Mineral Resources; A
  Series of Studies by Specialists, 1st ed. N. Y. McGraw Book Co. 1920.
 Coal. By G. S. Rice and F. F. Grout. pp. 22–54.

Suffern, A. E.
 Conciliation and Arbitration in the Coal Industry of America. Boston.
  Houghton Mifflin Co. 1915. 376 pp.

Survey Graphic. New York
 Coal Number. April, 1922.

United Mine Workers of America, District No. 2
 Facts! Clearfield, Pa. 1921. 16 pp.
 Government of Coal. Clearfield, Pa. 1921. 24 pp.
 Miners' Program. Clearfield, Pa. 1921. 6 pp.
 Why the Miners' Program? Clearfield, Pa. 1921. 10 pp.

United Mine Workers of America. Nationalization Research Committee
 Compulsory Information in Coal; a Fact-Finding Agency. Clearfield, Pa. John
  Brophy, President, U. M. W. of A., District No. 2. 1922. 28 pp.

U. S. Bituminous Coal Commission
 Majority and Minority Reports. Wash. Govt. Printing Office. 1920. 120 pp.

U. S. Congress. House. Committee on Labor
 **Investigation of Wages and Working Conditions in the Coal-Mining Indus-
  try.** Hearings on H. R. 11022. Wash. Govt. Printing Office. 1922. Vol. 1. 443

pp. Nolan Committee on Bland Bill.

U. S. CONGRESS. SENATE. COMMITTEE ON EDUCATION AND LABOR
West Virginia Coal Fields. Hearings pursuant to S. Res. 80. Wash. Govt. Printing Office. 1921. 2 vols. (67th Cong., 1st Sess.)
West Virginia Coal Fields. Personal views of Senator Kenyon and views of Senators Sterling, Phipps, and Warren. Wash. Govt. Printing Office. 1922. 30 pp. (67th Cong., 2d Sess. S. Report No. 457.)

U. S. CONGRESS. SENATE. COMMITTEE ON INTERSTATE COMMERCE
Increased Price of Coal. Hearings Before a Subcommittee Pursuant to S. Res. 126. Wash. Govt. Printing Office. 1919. 4 vols. (66th Cong., 1st Sess.) Frelinghuysen Committee.

U. S. CONGRESS. SENATE. COMMITTEE ON MANUFACTURES
Publication of Production and Profits in Coal. Hearings on S. 4828. Wash. Govt. Printing Office. 1921. 3 vols. (66th Cong., 3d Sess.) La Follette Committee.

U. S. CONGRESS. SELECT COMMITTEE ON RECONSTRUCTION AND PRODUCTION
Reconstruction and Production. Hearings pursuant to S. Res. 350. Wash. Govt. Printing Office. 1921. 3 vols. (66th Cong., 3d Sess.)

U. S. FEDERAL TRADE COMMISSION
Cost Reports. Coal. June 30, 1919. Wash. Govt. Printing Office. 1919–1921.
Report ... on Anthracite and Bituminous Coal. Wash. Govt. Printing Office. 1917. 420 pp.

U. S. GEOLOGICAL SURVEY
Mineral Resources of the United States. Wash. Govt. Printing Office. 1881–date.

Weekly Report of Production. Wash. Geological Survey. 1917–date.

U. S. IMMIGRATION COMMISSION
Reports; Immigrants in Industries. Wash. Govt. Printing Office. 1911. Vols. 6, 7, 16.

WARNE, F. J.
Coal-Mine Workers; a Study in Labor Organization. N. Y. Longmans, Green & Co. 1905. 252 pp.

WEBB, SIDNEY and BEATRICE
History of Trade Unionism. Rev. ed. extended to 1920. N. Y. Longmans, Green & Co. 1920. 784 pp.

WEBB, SIDNEY
Story of the Durham Miners (1662–1921). London. Fabian Society. 1921. 145 pp.

COAL INDUSTRY—PERIODICALS

Coal Age. (Weekly.) McGraw-Hill Publishing Co. N. Y. 10th Ave. and 36th St. C. E. Lesher, editor.

Coal Review. (Weekly.) Official organ of National Coal Association. Wash., D. C., Commercial National Bank Bldg., 14th and G Sts. John B. Pratt, editor.

United Mine Workers' Journal. (Bi-monthly.) United Mine Workers of America. Merchants Bank Bldg. Indianapolis. Ellis Searles, editor.

Lector House believes that a society develops through a two-fold approach of continuous learning and adaptation, which is derived from the study of classic literary works spread across the historic timeline of literature records. Therefore, we aim at reviving, repairing and redeveloping all those inaccessible or damaged but historically as well as culturally important literature across subjects so that the future generations may have an opportunity to study and learn from past works to embark upon a journey of creating a better future.

This book is a result of an effort made by Lector House towards making a contribution to the preservation and repair of original ancient works which might hold historical significance to the approach of continuous learning across subjects.

HAPPY READING & LEARNING!

LECTOR HOUSE
LECTOR HOUSE LLP
E-MAIL: lectorpublishing@gmail.com